STORIES

The Redemption of One Man's Wounded Sexuality

STORIES

The Redemption of One Man's Wounded Sexuality

Tony Ingrassia

Copyright © 2004 by Tony Ingrassia

All rights reserved. No part of this publication may be reproduced in any form without written permission.

Unless otherwise indicated, all scripture quotations are taken from the *Holy Bible,* New International Version®. NIV®. Copyright© 1973, 1978, 1984 by the International Bible Society.

All quotations attributed to *"Strong's Concordance"* are taken from *Strong's Exhaustive Concordance of the Bible,* World Bible Publishers, Iowa City, Iowa.

ISBN # 0-9678350-8-9

For more information contact:
   Tony Ingrassia at **tony@powerofpurity.org**

Table of Contents

Introduction 7

Section 1 — The Descending Journey & Bondage

Chapter 1   The Surgeon's Scalpel 15

Chapter 2   Magazines & Books 19

Chapter 3   Attitudes & Words 23

Chapter 4   Masturbation, Bents, & Addiction 29

Chapter 5   Seductive Women & the "Vibe" 33

Chapter 6   Deeds in Darkness 39

Chapter 7   Spiritual Awakening 45

Chapter 8   My First Girlfriend, the Tasmanian Devil & the Cycle . .49

Chapter 9   My Pastor & My Girlfriend 53

Chapter 10 My Pastor & "Thou Art the Man" 57

Chapter 11 The Golden Boy 61

Chapter 12 Canaan 65

Chapter 13 Public Shame 69

Chapter 14 Sheri 73

Chapter 15 A Shaky Foundation 77

Chapter 16	Unrealistic Expectations	.81
Chapter 17	A Head-on Collision	.85
Chapter 18	Emotional Revolt	.89
Chapter 19	Unfaithfulness & Betrayal	.93

Section 2 — The Ascending Journey & Freedom

Chapter 20	Divine Desperation	99
Chapter 21	Inner Voices & the Heavy Hand of God	105
Chapter 22	Confession	109
Chapter 23	Submission to Authority	115
Chapter 24	Therapy	119
Chapter 25	The Small Group	125
Chapter 26	The Vow	129
Chapter 27	Embracing Pain & Psalm 131	135
Chapter 28	Physical Pain & a Taste of Freedom	141
Chapter 29	Two Steps Forward & One Step Back	147
Chapter 30	Restitution	151
Chapter 31	Therapy II & a Crown of Thorns	155
Chapter 32	A Heart of Flesh & an Eye of Suspicion	161
Chapter 33	The Vow II	165
Chapter 34	The Schedule & the Fury of Hell	169
Chapter 35	The Power of Prayer	175
Chapter 36	Joel 2 & a New Beginning	181
Chapter 37	Divine Sex & the Future	185
Chapter 38	Enemy Fire	189
Chapter 39	Narrow is the Path	195
Chapter 40	Sheri's Voice	203

Introduction

Why in the world would I want to write a book like this? Why would I be willing to reveal and discuss the most shameful, embarrassing, and troubled areas of my life? Why should I expose my deepest intimacies and failures? In short, because I believe God wants me to, and because I felt compelled to write for three specific reasons.

First, I believe that we are in a very real battle, with very real enemies, and very high stakes. I believe the devil and his cohorts want nothing more than to hurt the heart of God, primarily by destroying the lives of those whom God loves, namely you and me. I know beyond a shadow of a doubt that the primary way the enemy tried to destroy my life was through my misguided and wounded sexuality. From a very early age, as you'll see through the "stories" you are about to read, I suffered a natural weakness in the sexual area of my life. This weakness quickly progressed from a struggle, to a stronghold, to an addiction, and then to a bondage that would hold me for years like a prisoner in invisible chains. Through the dark and painful process of struggling for so many years with my sexuality, I believe the enemy tried to destroy everything of significance in my life, including my marriage, my family, my ministry, and my very life. But there is good news, and that is that if you are a prisoner, you can be set free. In a central passage about Jesus' ministry — the very passage He spoke when He came out of the wilderness after being tempted by the devil, and began His public ministry — He reveals the reason for His calling and the primary purpose of His ministry.

> The Spirit of the Lord is on me, because he has anointed me
> to preach good news to the poor. He has sent me to proclaim
> freedom for the prisoners and recovery of sight for the blind,

8 Stories: The Redemption of One Man's Wounded Sexuality

to release the oppressed, to proclaim the year of the Lord's favor. Luke 4:18–19

As you'll see, through the incredibly difficult and dark valley God required me to walk through, He proved to me that He really can set prisoners free, and through the unexpected way in which He can bring life out of death through the mystery of the gospel, He slowly began to redeem my broken life and sexuality back to Himself. What brings absolute delight to my heart today is the hope that God can take the primary way the devil tried to destroy my life — my wounded sexuality — and instead, through the story of my redemption, bring destruction upon the enemy and his kingdom of darkness. That's the first reason I wanted to write this book: to get back at the devil for all the harm, pain, and destruction he tried to bring into my life. My hope is that God can use my story to help free other men from their chains of darkness, and in so doing unleash massive destruction upon the enemy's vile kingdom.

Secondly, I believe there is a desperate need for discussion related to this taboo subject, especially in the Church. I believe there is no greater issue central to what it means to be a man, or to masculinity, than our sexuality. The relevance of this issue and the struggle it represents in the lives of most men is almost universal, yet it seems to be one of the most neglected and avoided topics of discussion, even in the Church. Why is this? I believe that the Church should offer the greatest attention and care for people in the areas where they struggle the most, where the rubber really meets the road. My suspicion is that for most men such severe struggles would include the subject of their sexuality. As I have shared my story with a number of men, I've been amazed by the universality of this struggle, and the depth of the hunger within men to find freedom and relief from the silent and hidden shame of their weaknesses and failures. I believe many men, including men in the Church, are deeply struggling and suffering in quiet desperation with bondages and invisible chains holding them captive in dark and hidden places. I believe if we could somehow take an average church in America and cut it in half to see what's inside, just as you might cut a watermelon in half, we would be shocked to know how deeply so many men are struggling with bondages to lust, pornography, masturbation, affairs, and perversions, among many other strongholds.

Recently, I shared my story with the pastor of a large local church, and as I did he confided with me that he has struggled deeply with this area of his life. He struggles alone because he doesn't know where or how to find help, as he has to be careful to maintain his public image. When I was in a foreign country on a mission trip, I felt impressed to share my story with a full-time missionary working there. As I did, he suddenly burst into tears and pleaded with me to help him. He confessed his deep struggles with overwhelming sexual thoughts and feelings toward people around him. He said he felt alone in his struggle and had nowhere to go for help. These are examples of godly men who have devoted their lives to serving God, and whose ministries God has used and blessed greatly. Yet, apparently it's possible for a man of God to suffer deeply with his sexuality.

As I began to research the extent and effects of pornography in our society, I was amazed at what I found. In lieu of providing a long list of quotes and statistics, let me simply share that "adult" video and bookstores in the United States now outnumber McDonald's restaurants[1], and Americans spend over eight billion dollars per year on pornography, which is an amount larger than Hollywood's annual domestic box office receipts and larger than all the revenues generated by rock and country music recordings[2]. It's as if we as a people have erected the false god of a giant golden penis, and our entire society is bowing down in worship. I fear that the reality of this hideous plague is not limited to just our humanistic society, but has also infiltrated the Church, and is effectively neutralizing many Christian men from the status of "Warrior Poet" to the position of "P.O.W." — prisoner of war. I believe it's time for the Church to attack this issue head-on, and move it from the place of silence and hidden shadows where it currently lurks, and expose it to the full "light" of truth. We need to create the opportunities for discussions, small groups, meetings, and forums where men can begin to find honest answers for the difficult questions they struggle with, and begin to move from bondage to freedom. My hope is that my story can in some small way provide an impetus for men to relate to as they begin to face this issue more honestly than ever before. We desperately need help; we desperately need each other; and that's the second reason I wanted to write this book: to get the issue in front of us, and to give Jesus the chance to do what He does best — set captives free.

The third and final reason I wrote this book is because something deep in my heart longs to be "known." I believe that God created us primarily for the purpose of relationship. We are created to know, and to be known. We are to know God, and we are to be known by God. We are to know others, and we are to be known by others. We are called to relationship, and we are called to be known. As I have grown through the redemptive process of

God's work in my life, I find a strange and growing desire in my heart to be known in a deeper way by those around me. One of the things that saddens me is how little I know of the people around me, and how little I feel they know of me. I'm talking about the people I see every week in my circles of relationship, and the people who are supposed to be the closest in my life. I mean really — how well do you truly know the people around you? Do you know their deepest thoughts and desires? Do you know the stories of their lives? Do you know what their deepest struggles are, their deepest hopes, and their deepest fears? I think it's really sad how little we know of the people around us, and how little they know of us. And that's the final reason I wanted to write this book: I wanted people to know who I really am — the good, the bad, and the ugly — and my hope is that as I continue to grow as a person, that I can continue to learn about and know the people around me in a deeper way than ever before.

I encourage you to read my "stories" with an open heart, and as you do, my hope is that you might reflect upon your own life through the template of how God has worked in my life as He has slowly redeemed my wounded sexuality. My hope is that you will let God speak into the deepest places of your heart through my "stories." As you read, contemplate what God might be asking of you in this important area of life, and what it would take for you to honor Him in a greater way through the expression of your own sexuality.

I struggled deeply as I wrote certain things herein about other people — especially my father — because in so doing I often exposed negative character traits. The dilemma arose because I felt compelled to tell my own story, and in order to do so honestly I was required to reveal certain details about others that are significant pieces to the puzzle of my own life. I sincerely believe my father loved me, and the rest of his children, to the best of his ability, and I believe he did the best job as a father that he could do within the context of the resources that were available to him at the time. In sharing such things it is not my intent to blame my father or anyone else for my own mistakes, or for my own sins. I know that one day I will stand before God to give an account for my life, and on that day I will not be able to give any excuses or blame anyone else for the things I have done wrong. I will answer to God alone, and I will not have anyone to point a finger at except for myself. I share these stories, therefore, to simply help others understand the influences that contributed to the development of sinful tendencies and patterns in my life.

While it is true that my father negatively influenced the person I was becoming as a young man, it is also true that he blessed my life in many different ways. He was always a very hard worker and faithfully provided for his family. In addition to his full-time job, he almost always worked a part-time job. I even remember a time when he had three jobs at once. He occasionally played games with his children — like kickball, corkball, and wiffleball — and he took us on various outings over the years like the state fair, picnics, and vacations at the lake. I think the greatest gift my father gave me was the gift of the outdoors. He loved to hunt and went out of his way to include me in his hunting expeditions since I was a young child. I remember going rabbit hunting with him before I could even carry a gun. I would walk along behind him, jump on brush piles to chase the rabbits out, and help him carry the rabbits he killed. Over the years hunting became my own passion, and we spent endless hours together on various hunting trips. In fact, the time we spent together hunting came to define our relationship, and apart from hunting together, my father and I had very little in common. For all these things I am deeply grateful to the memory of my father.

---

1 From the article, "Battle Plan Against Pornography" found at *The Parsonage* — www.parsonage.org, a ministry of Focus on the Family.

2 Eric Schlosser, "The Business of Pornography," *U.S. News and World Report*, February 10, 1997.

SECTION 1

THE DESCENDING
JOURNEY & BONDAGE

CHAPTER 1

THE SURGEON'S SCALPEL

When I was 15 years old, I had one of the most painful experiences of my life. I woke up in the middle of the night with a dull but persistent pain in my abdomen. There was enough discomfort to wake me but not enough for me to become alarmed. I tossed and turned the rest of the night in that mysterious place of being half awake and half asleep at the same time. The next morning, while getting ready for school, I remember standing in the kitchen fixing my lunch and telling my mom I didn't feel well. She could apparently discern I was telling the truth because she suggested I stay home for the day. Normally I would have jumped at the chance to miss a day of school but, for some reason beyond my memory, I wanted to go to school that day; perhaps it was a test I didn't want to miss, or an activity I wanted to participate in, so off to school I went.

The pain persisted during the bus ride to school and seemed to worsen as I walked from my locker to my first class. The more I moved, the sharper the pain became, and I soon noticed it was becoming isolated to the right side of my abdomen. I started to feel nauseous sometime during the course of that class, so I raised my hand to be excused. I had that terrible feeling you have right before you're going to vomit, so I quickly walked down the hallway to the nearest restroom. As I stood over the toilet with my hands against the wall, waves of nausea swept over me, and suddenly everything went black.

What happened next is difficult to describe because it was an ethereal

15

kind of experience. It felt as though I was suspended deep in a body of water completely surrounded by darkness. As I wondered where I was and what was happening to me, I slowly became aware of a dim light in the distance. Sensing that I was drifting toward the light, the darkness that engulfed me began to surrender its hold on me, and shades of black slowly faded to shades of gray. My eyelids felt like they weighed a thousand pounds each, and as I labored to open them I became aware of the horrible pain on the back of my head. After being in a kind of haze for what seemed like a prolonged period of time, I gradually focused on the ceiling, and I realized I was flat on my back in the middle of the bathroom. Apparently I had passed out and clobbered my head during the fall.

I tried to reach for the back of my head, but seemed unable to move. As I wondered how long I had been lying there, I slowly found the strength to get up and make my way to the nurse's office. The school nurse called my mom, who promptly came and picked me up, and then took me directly to the doctor's office. By the time we got there the pain of my throbbing head seemed insignificant to the almost unbearable and stabbing pain in my side. After a short wait in the examination room, the doctor came in, felt around on my abdomen, asked a few questions, and quickly delivered his diagnosis: "This kid has appendicitis! Take him directly to the hospital. We have to operate immediately!" My mom rushed me to the hospital, and without delay I was prepared for surgery. The doctor arrived, and I remember being wheeled into the cold and uninviting operating room, with its bright lights and cold stainless steel tables. The strangers who swarmed around me looked more like aliens than people because of the funny clothes and masks they wore. As the anesthesiologist placed a strange mask over my face, she told me to count backwards from ten to one, and as I obeyed, it felt like I was falling in slow motion back into the dark pool of water.

The next thing I remember was trying to wake up in the recovery room. I felt so cold I was shivering. There was a young nurse near my bed, and with groggy words I tried to tell her I was freezing. Moments later, as she covered me with warm blankets, I felt like I was watching an angel take care of me, and I instantly became enraptured with her beauty. Apparently the gatekeeper of my mouth — who would normally prohibit the escape of such embarrassing honesty — was still sleeping, as Mr. Libido took over and I suddenly blurted out to my newfound angel, "You are so beautiful! I can't believe how beautiful you are!" With my awkward announcement the nurse first looked surprised, then embarrassed, but then she laughed and thanked me for the compliment as she patted me on the face and walked away. Even now I feel a sense of embarrassment as I remember what I said to her, and something in my heart feels sadness for a young boy whose first impulse in such circumstances was directed toward the beauty of a woman. From the time the doctor first saw me to the time he cut me with his scalpel was less than two hours. He said later he barely reached my appendix in time, as it was on the verge of bursting.

Like a prophetic mirror, there are images in this story from long ago that would somehow come to fruition in my future. There's the image of a young boy who had something go wrong deep on the inside — something foreign to his health and the way God had created him, and something that would even lead to death if it wasn't addressed. There's the image of a boy who needed to be rescued. He needed someone to do for him what he could never do for himself. In order to be saved from his dilemma, the boy needed to submit to a master surgeon's wisdom and touch. Finally, there's the image of the doctor's chosen method of healing that seems a cruel irony: to heal the boy the doctor would, in a sense, first hurt him further. In order to restore him, the doctor would assault the boy with a sharp scalpel, and cause even more pain by cutting deeply into him.

Chapter 2
Magazines & Books

 I remember finding my father's pornography when I was a young boy. I think I was 10 or 11 years old. He had a stack of magazines hidden in his bedroom closet. I can't remember how or why I found them. I was probably snooping around where little boys weren't supposed to. After my discovery, I snuck into their bedroom as often as I could to look through the magazines. Both of my parents were frequently gone from home at the same time, and the solitude of such moments provided the perfect opportunity for me to peek at the colorful pictures. I can remember lying on their bed with numerous magazines open at the same time all around me. I even remember taking the great risk at times of peeking while my mother was at home. If she went downstairs to do the laundry, I could quietly, like a secret agent on a mission, sneak a peep at the magazines because I knew she would be busy for an extended period of time. In retrospect, I can't believe I was brave enough — or stupid enough — to risk looking while my mother was at home. I can only imagine my willingness to take such a risk reveals something of an almost desperation that existed in me at the time. Apparently there were times I wanted to look so badly that the risk of being caught was worth the opportunity to feed my hungry eyes.

As if the influence of these magazines was not enough, I also found a dirty book in my father's dresser drawer. I remember the names of the author and the book, but think it best not to reveal them. It was a book written by a woman concerning her many sexual experiences as a prostitute. Among many others, it explicitly recounted her exploits with men, other women, groups of men, young boys, and even animals. The scenes of her adventures included bedrooms, hotels, swimming pools, automobiles, and airports. When I found the book, I remember consuming it with passion. As my eyes pored over the pages, they soaked up the words and stories in much the same way a new sponge might soak up a spill. I remember reading the book repeatedly. I read and reread — time and again — passages that were especially appealing to me. Like a powerful magnet, it seemed as if I could almost always feel the pages and words pulling me back to them, and I would anxiously wait for the next opportunity to rendezvous with them.

Until I found the book, the magazines had held a place of growing power in my young life. In fact, they were so powerful they even commanded me to obey them when my common sense told me I shouldn't — like when I risked peeking even when my mother was at home. However, when I found the book, it quickly supplanted the magazines' place of power in my young heart, and assumed a place of preeminence. From that time forward I looked at the magazines occasionally, but I spent far more time reading and rereading the book. I can only assume the stories related in the book — offered in such graphic and intimate detail — did more to quicken my young mind than the pictures in the magazines. It's as if the magazines submitted appetizers for my developing heart to taste — a single frame taken from a single moment frozen in time and offered in the form of a still photograph; while the stories in the book invited me to a veritable banquet — like a feature film presented in vivid color and surround sound on the big screen of my mind. No wonder the book became the new emperor in my heart. It brought to life, in a sense, the still images I had been watching for so long in the magazines. It allowed them to breathe, move, and talk within the context of stories. It gave them life and allowed them to do things I had never imagined people doing. Like a young child looking with fascination at a fish tank for the very first time, it allowed me to look into a world I never knew existed, and it gave me a front-row seat for the show.

As I reflect on my childhood, I'm amazed at the power of these memories. It's as though my mind was seared at the time with a red-hot branding iron. Even now, over 30 years later, I can instantly recall in graphic detail lewd cartoons from the magazines and the various stories I read in the book. It's as though they are stored away in a corner closet somewhere in my mind — stuffed and bulging on top of one another — and should I choose to open the door to that corner of my mind, they all come tumbling out again at my feet. As soon as I look down and see one of them, it instantly comes back to life in the theater of my mind, and then, like a giant game of dominoes, the memories parade in one after the other. I believe a young boy's heart is like a soft piece of clay, upon which exposure to pornography can leave a permanent impression. As I remember the strange power the magazines and books exerted upon me, and as I remember my willingness to take such risks to peek at them, I see the seeds being planted in me as a young boy that would take root and grow as I would become a man.

CHAPTER 3

Attitudes
& Words

One of the greatest ways my father harmed me was through the example and demonstration of his sexuality. Through a natural process, I was slowly over time soaking up his attitudes and words, and he was teaching me many lessons I didn't even know I was learning[1]. He was teaching me what it meant to be a man. He was teaching me how a man expresses his sexuality. He was teaching me the kinds of attitudes I should have toward women, the ways I should treat women, and the things I should say to women. He was teaching me that sex is the thing that makes a man's soul feel alive — that sex is the cistern a man could drink from to quench his thirsty soul — that sex is the lesser god who is worthy of my devotion. Although I recall many examples of my father's attitudes and words regarding sex, I'll share only a few.

My father made almost endless lewd and suggestive comments. We might be riding in the car and have a woman stop next to us at a stoplight. It wasn't unusual for him to gawk in such a manner that even made me feel uncomfortable as a young boy. He often offered words that were consistent with the stature of his heart at the moment, typically pointing out in a suggestive or lewd way the woman's beauty or some particular feature about her that he was taken with. A woman — or girl — could have been walking down the street, riding a bicycle, or working in her yard. She may have been at the park, in the store, or at the doctor's office. It didn't matter when or where she appeared; my father quickly noticed her presence and drank deeply with his

23

eyes. The other convenient and consistent purveyor, offering an endless supply of tasty morsels for one who might be hungry for such things, was the television. It seemed impossible to watch television with my father, whether it was Hee-Haw, Laugh In, or whatever else might be on, without his noticing the beautiful, voluptuous, or scantily-clad women. Regardless of who was there to hear his inappropriate comments, he would typically present them with seeming delight. It was clear that such things quickened his soul and gave him a sense of being more alive.

When I was a young boy my father went rabbit hunting with his buddies almost every Sunday during rabbit season. One of the greatest blessings my father gave me as a child was the opportunity to be included in these expeditions. I was typically the only youngster among a group of several men on these trips, and it wasn't uncommon for us to ride 3 or 4 hours in the car to our hunting spot. I mostly listened while the men talked and joked with one another, and while it wasn't unusual for coarse or dirty things to be said among the group, one specific incident stands out in my mind. This one particular man who hunted with us for a period of time seemed exceptionally lewd and immoral. He told nasty jokes and freely disclosed various episodes regarding his infidelities. On one particular trip this man began talking to my father about a woman he knew who was apparently available for such extramarital activities. He was willing to set my father up with this woman and encouraged him to take advantage of the opportunity. I remember him saying it would be good for my father to rendezvous with this woman, and although they talked in hushed voices in an attempt to keep me from hearing what they were saying, I could still hear the conversation in the close confines of the car.

That evening, my father pulled me aside and gave me a stern warning to never repeat any of the things I happened to hear on the hunting trips. He told me that if I ever said anything, I wouldn't be allowed to go along anymore. I nodded my head in assent, but remember feeling very disturbed. I was angry with the other man for saying such things to my father, and angry with my father for entertaining such a discussion. I was old enough to know what they were talking about, and I found the thought of my father doing such a thing very upsetting. Although I was so upset regarding the matter, I felt powerless to say anything to my father because of my fear of him, and I didn't want to jeopardize my standing in the group of men by saying something my father didn't want me to say. At such a young age, I simply didn't have the resources to know what to do with all the confusing thoughts and feelings that were swirling around inside of me. Consequently, I never said anything to my mother or anyone else, and although my father was never unfaithful to my mother that I know of, reflecting on such memories gives rise to suspicion in my heart.

My father's apparent preoccupation with sexual thoughts and his suggestive comments continued for many years. I heard him say — on many occasions — unbelievably inappropriate things to other women. It didn't seem to matter what the occasion was or who was present. He offered his lewd thoughts and comments to these women even in front of their husbands, in front of my mother, and in front of children. I remember feeling so many times — even as a youngster — a sense of embarrassment and discomfort when he conducted himself in such a manner. In retrospect, I think he was able to get away with such behavior because it was typically offered in a kind of joking or teasing way. People normally dismissed his comments with a kind of nervous laughter, and then changed the subject to something more appropriate. After I got married, my father even made inappropriate comments to my wife. Much to my own shame, I normally ignored these situations by saying or doing nothing. In so doing I believe I deeply failed my wife, because I should have honored her by protecting her from the indignity of such comments. She was deeply bothered by these situations, yet I felt paralyzed in my inability to do anything about them. I was accustomed to my father's behavior and figured he would never change anyway, so I rationalized that it wouldn't matter if I confronted him. Only after I had been in therapy myself for an extended period of time did I begin to find the strength to confront my father about such things. I remember one such incident.

It occurred at the time the Hale Bopp comet was passing near planet Earth. The comet was a glorious sight — even through common binoculars — for an extended period of weeks. One evening my parents came over for dinner, and we all went outside after dark to view the comet. As we each took turns observing through the binoculars, my youngest son — who was just learning to talk — impatiently insisted, "I want to see boobs! I want to see boobs!" As we corrected him and explained the comet was called Hale Bopp — not Hale Boobs — my father quickly made a rude comment about his desire to see some "boobs" also. When we went back into the house, I asked my father if I could speak with him privately. We went into a rear bedroom of the house, and I told him I thought his comments were rude and inappropriate. He seemed surprised and defended his behavior by saying he was only kidding around. I told him again I didn't think such coarse jesting was appropriate, and I asked him not to make such comments in front of my family. I told him I thought such comments demonstrated a bad example to the children and disrespected the women who were present. He said he didn't think it was such a big deal, but he would try to be more sensitive in the future. It wasn't a big event in and of itself, but it was significant because it represented a kind of first step for me in my attempt to establish some proper boundaries with my father.

---

1 In his book, *Bringing Up Boys, Dr.* James Dobson writes:

> Now I want to focus on the two primary ways a dad's influence is transmitted at home, beginning with modeling. If character training is a primary goal of parenting, and I believe it is, then the best way to instill it is through the demeanor and behavior of a father. Identification with him is a far more efficient teacher than lecturing, scolding, punishing, bribing, and cajoling. Boys watch their dads intently, noting every minor detail of be havior and values. It is probably true in your home, too. Your sons will imitate much of what you do. If you blow up regularly and insult your wife, your boys will treat their mother and other females disrespectfully. If you drink to excess, your kids will be at risk for chemical substance abuse. If you curse or smoke or fight with your coworkers, your boys will probably follow suit. If you are selfish or mean or angry, you'll see those characteristics displayed in the next generation.
>
> Fortunately, the converse is also true. If you are honest, trustworthy, caring, loving, self-disciplined, and God-fearing, your boys will be influenced by those traits as they age. If you are deeply committed to Jesus Christ and live by biblical principles, your children will probably follow in your footsteps. So much depends on what they observe in you, for better or for worse.
>
> Someone said, "I'd rather see a sermon than hear one." There is truth to this statement. Children may not remember what you say, but they are usually impacted for life by what you do.
>
> *Bringing Up Boys,* Dr. James Dobson, Tyndale House Publishers, Inc., 2001, page 69.

The point Dr. Dobson is making in these observations was dramatically illustrated to me once through the behavior of my then 7-year-old son, Sammy. One Saturday afternoon I took Sammy and one of his buddies to a church dinner and carnival. As the three of us walked around the fair, I discovered a booth selling beautiful sterling silver jewelry from Greece. Since my wife Sheri loves silver, I picked out a beautiful necklace and purchased it for her as a surprise. We continued on our way, and the boys systematically collected various prizes as they played a variety of games and challenges on the fairway. As we neared the end of the afternoon, and it was almost time to leave, Sammy had one ticket left to redeem for the prize of his choice. I thought for sure he would go for one more squirt gun, since his friend had a total of three, and Sammy had only added two to his growing stockpile of booty. As he reviewed his many choices — a rubber ball, a whistle, a plastic snake, a slinky, an airplane, a car, or a pair of glasses complete with attached fake nose and mustache, among other options — his friend kept encouraging him to choose the ultimate prize: another squirt gun! "Come on, Sam! Get the squirt gun! Get the orange one! I've got three and you've only got two! Get the orange squirt gun and we'll both have three!" As Sammy continued to review his options from the colorful items spread before him, he suddenly asked the lady in charge, completely unsolicited by me or anyone else, if he could trade his last ticket for one of the bracelets in a small box on the back corner of the table. The lady was obviously surprised, and inquired why in the world a little boy would want such a prize. He looked directly at the lady and said without hesitation, "I want to get a bracelet for my mom!" The lady commented how sweet and thoughtful he was, and told Sammy she thought his mommy was lucky to have such a special little boy. He proceeded to make his selection, and as we walked away, while I felt a sense of pride in the stature of my young son's heart, I also had a sense of trepidation as I realized that he was watching and learning from my example how to treat the women in his life. We made our way home, and my wife Sheri became the proud recipient of one beautiful sterling silver necklace, and in my opinion, an even more beautiful toy bracelet!

CHAPTER 4

MASTURBATION, BENTS & ADDICTION

I believe I was 11 years old when I began to masturbate. I remember experiencing feelings of pleasure when I touched myself, but that was nothing in comparison to the powerful sensation I felt when I had my first orgasm. It was unlike anything I had ever felt or experienced. After the discovery of this newfound source of gratification, I actually had a reason to touch myself. I quickly learned that this feeling of intense pleasure could be replicated over and over, and thus began an activity in my life that I would struggle with for years to come. It's as though the magazines and books had found a strategic ally in their war against me, and their powerful grip on my young soul was strengthened.

I remember the first time I ejaculated. Prior to that I had several orgasms, but never with such a surprising conclusion. I remember feeling scared to death. I had no idea what had happened or why. I actually thought I had broken my body somehow, and that something was wrong. I wanted to tell my mother about it because I was scared of what might happen. I thought maybe I needed to go to the hospital to have something fixed, but I couldn't bring myself to tell my mother. I can only imagine I had an intuitive sense of shame, and knew I would have to somehow explain what I was doing and why I was doing it. Apparently this sense of shame was very powerful, because in spite of the fear that I had damaged my body and needed to go to the hospital, I still did not tell anyone what had happened. Even worse, in the days that followed I continued to masturbate. Although I was

29

afraid of what my body was doing, and thought I was harming myself by this activity, I simply couldn't stop.

In retrospect, I believe these events were the early signs of what was already becoming a sexual addiction in my life. I recognize that adolescent boys masturbate, and the experts say this should be considered normal behavior. However, I believe the path I was on was abnormal, and that I was over sexualized at a very young age. The intensity of sexual energy swirling around me, the amount of time I spent looking at the magazines and books, the time I spent thinking about such things, and the self discovery of masturbation at such an early age are all evidence to me of an inordinate sexual awakening. Webster's defines an addiction as "the condition of being a slave to a habit." I think it's fair to say that I was already in bondage to a kind of sexual slavery, evidenced by things like my willingness to risk looking at the magazines and books even when my mother was at home, and my willingness to continue masturbating even though I was afraid I was hurting myself. There was a kind of powerful master beginning to rule my life, and whenever he called to me I seemed powerless to do anything other than obey.

In my own words, for me, an addiction is when something controls me more than I control it. I'm continuously amazed as I observe, not only in myself but also the people around me, the obvious propensity human beings have to deny their addictions. In a discussion I had with a friend of mine who has smoked cigarettes for years, he insisted he could stop smoking anytime he wanted. I therefore challenged him to stop smoking if it would be so easy. When he sensed how serious I was, he became uneasy with the prospect of quitting, and was forced to admit he wasn't sure he would be able to quit. In the normal ebb and flow of life, he was able to deceive himself into believing that he was in control of the cigarettes, but confronted by the strength of my words, he was forced to admit the truth. We're quick to believe our own lies, as the Apostle John said, "If we claim to be without sin, we deceive ourselves and the truth is not in us" (I John 1:8).

On a recent business trip, I was working with a man who easily weighed more than four-hundred pounds. One night as we were having dinner, he explained to me that he was so overweight because he was so busy with work. I inquired further. He explained that the requirements of his hectic schedule didn't allow time for him to eat healthy meals, so he was forced to eat fast food and junk food on the run. Apparently it was easier for him to blame his obvious weight problem on his busy work schedule than to blame it on himself. Isn't it amazing how we can justify to ourselves why we do the things we do? And I'm just as guilty! I spent many years denying and explaining away my sexual history, and only through an extensive and profoundly difficult counseling process was I able to begin to admit to myself that I had a sexual addiction that had roots all the way into my childhood[1].

I've come to believe that every person has a natural "bent" toward certain sinful behaviors and addictions. If a person was to take a young tree, about the size of your thumb, and bend it over and tie it down with a rope for the next 5 years, the tree would literally begin to grow in that position. If you were to cut the rope at the end of those 5 years, guess what? The tree would stay in the bent position, because it would have been trained to grow that way. The very grain of wood on the inside of the tree would have been programmed to assume the posture the rope had required of it 5 years earlier. In much the same way, a variety of influences can predispose people to have certain "bents" or tendencies toward sin. Some people are bent toward alcoholism, others toward drugs or homosexuality. Some are bent toward the excessive use of power, food, or work. Whatever our bent, it represents our autonomous tendency to manage life and make it work on our own terms; it's our attempt to find soothing relief and freedom from the pain life has to offer. For me, I believe I was vulnerable from childhood toward a weakness in the sexual area of my life, and I believe my sexual addiction began at a very early age.

---

1 Sexual addictions that begin in childhood are recognized and documented by such experts as Dr. Victor B. Cline, a licensed clinical psychologist and noted sex therapist in Salt Lake City, Utah. He has treated hundreds of male cases for sexual addiction and compulsions. The following excerpts are taken from an article written by Dr. Cline entitled, *Treatment and Healing of Sexual and Pornographic Addictions,* and can be found at www.moralityinmedia.org/pornsEffects/vbctreat.htm.

> I found that nearly all of my adult sexual addicts' problems started with porn exposure in childhood or adolescence (8 years and older). The typical pattern was exposure to mild porn early with increased frequency of exposure and eventual later addiction. This was nearly always accompanied by masturbation.
>
> I found that once addicted, whether to just the pornography or the later pattern of sexual acting out, they really lost their "free-agency." It was like a drug addiction. And in this case their drug was sex. They could not stop the pattern of their behavior, no matter how high-risk for them it was.

32 STORIES: THE REDEMPTION of ONE MAN's WOUNDED SEXUALITY

In addition, the following excerpt is taken from Dr. Cline's article, *Pornography's Effects on Adults and Children,* and can be found at www.moralityinmedia.org/pornsEffects/clineart.htm.

I find in my clinical practice a spill-over effect where pornography used by adults very frequently gets into the hands of children living in the home or neighborhood. This can cause extremely negative consequences.

In his book, *Pure Desire,* (page 69) author Ted Roberts says:

We are awash in a sea of pornography, and the waves are only getting higher. The average age of a first-time viewer of pornography is now down to 11. It will drop even lower in the future because of the flood of porn that is coming through the Internet. Bondage to pornography is seldom something that develops later in life. Usually the seed is planted at a very early age, and by the time of young adulthood its tentacles have been deeply rooted into the person's mind.

Chapter 5

Seductive Women & the "Vibe"

When I was 14 years old, two different seductive women came into my life. The first one was a young lady I was around on an ongoing basis, who was 5 years older than me. One weekend I went on a short trip with several people, including this particular young lady. As we drove home, I fell asleep in the car. Although she was not driving, she was sitting in the front seat of the car, and I was sitting in the backseat with another person. I had a small throw blanket over me, and after some period of time I remember feeling stirred as if someone was trying to quietly wake me up. As I slowly opened my eyes, I realized this girl's arm was draped over the front seat in a way that would not create attention, and her arm was under my blanket as she gently caressed the inside of my thigh and leg with her hand. For a moment I thought she was joking, and I wondered what she was doing.

As she continued softly touching me, it slowly began to dawn on me what she was doing, and as it did the realization took my breath away. I suddenly felt paralyzed by the different feelings that flashed through me like lightning bolts, and the multitude of thoughts that raced through my mind. "What is she doing? Why is she doing this? She shouldn't be doing this! What if someone sees her touching me? What should I do?" I looked to the side and realized the person next to me was asleep, and since the driver of the car couldn't see what was happening, the whole event was apparently occurring in secrecy. She continued touching me in a way I had never been touched before, and as I submitted, a variety of conflicting thoughts and feelings — confusion, fear, and delight — swirled through my soul. But most of all, I remember how pleasing her touch was. As she continued to gently caress me, I can only imagine that the feelings awakened in me previously through the magazines and books were somehow being confirmed by my very first experience of intimate and sensual contact with another human being.

That was the first intimate contact I had with this particular young woman, and as I was around her on an ongoing basis, some other incidents also occurred, one of which stands out in my mind. One evening I was home alone when she stopped by. I remember sitting at the kitchen table as she stood behind me and began giving me a shoulder and backrub. It felt so good when she touched me, and in retrospect I believe, in a strange way, she was touching me with more than just her hands. It's as though something that was alive on the inside of her soul — a kind of sensual energy, or hungry and compelling desire — was touching something that had already been awakened deep inside my soul. Like the sea nymphs of Greek and Roman mythology, the siren song and invitation to sensual pleasure was calling my name and enticing me toward itself, and it would be years later that I would come to refer to this phenomenon as the "vibe."

The "vibe" is an aggressive and obvious sexual energy that seems to radiate like an aura around a person, which certain people around him or her can mysteriously sense. In the years to come, just like a radio that's tuned to a certain wavelength in order to send and receive signals, I would learn to sense the "vibe" from certain women around me, and be attracted to them accordingly. It became the most amazing phenomenon, but I could walk into a store, office, or restaurant and see a woman who was a complete stranger, and as our eyes met, I felt this overwhelming and intense attraction to her, and knew immediately that she was powerfully attracted to me. The "vibe" is like a mysterious and invisible force that somehow pulls two people toward one another like two strong magnets, and although I can't prove it, I suspect there are soulish and spiritual energies at work in such situations, enabling people with similar weaknesses and bents to find one another.

> See how you behaved in the valley; consider what you have done. You are a swift she-camel running here and there, a wild donkey accustomed to the desert, sniffing the wind in her craving — in her heat who can restrain her? Any males

that pursue her need not tire themselves; at mating time they will find her. Jeremiah 2:23–24

I learned to intuitively sense the "vibe" in certain women around me, and eventually learned to radiate it to the women around me in return. As I grew older, the "vibe" created significant problems in my life, because it enabled me to send and receive signals to and from the women around me who would be most responsive to my moral weakness. But my first experience with the "vibe," and the first time I sensed its enchanting voice calling my name, was through this particular young woman.

After she rubbed my shoulders for some time, she asked me if I wanted to switch places, and if I would give her a backrub. We switched positions, and I began to slowly and awkwardly rub her shoulders and neck. After several moments had passed, she told me the way I was touching her felt good, and she said I didn't have to just rub her shoulders, but I could go ahead and touch her anywhere else if I wanted to. Her intent was obvious, and I clearly understood what she wanted me to do, but for reasons I don't fully understand or remember, I did not touch her elsewhere. I can only imagine a sense of fear, and probably guilt, prevented me from doing so. Fear because I had never done anything like that before, and I really wasn't quite sure what to do, and guilt because she was the girlfriend of someone I knew, and I intuitively knew that touching her would constitute a betrayal of him.

In retrospect, I believe this girl had a seductive spirit about her at the time, and that she was seducing me with her words and actions. I don't know if she really liked me, or if she simply enjoyed teasing me and playing with me like a cat might play with a mouse it has caught and wounded. I'm quite sure her feeling of sensual titillation was heightened by my obvious inexperience and the sense of power she must have felt by being the aggressor. One thing is for sure though — she was clearly manipulating that particular situation and me.

The other seductive woman that came into my life was even older. In fact, she was married and had two children. Since they lived in a neighborhood near ours, I babysat for them occasionally. When she picked me up to baby-sit, we sometimes stopped at the store to do some shopping or to run some errands on the way. She was a stunningly beautiful woman who easily turned the heads of most of the men around her, and in a short matter of time I began to feel the same sensual energy between the two of us that I had already felt with the other young woman. As I got to know her a little better she began to frequently say and do suggestive things around me, and she talked to me at length while I sat and listened about how bad her marriage was, and how much she disliked her husband. One incident stands out in my mind.

One night she invited me to go to the drive-in with her and her two children. For whatever reason her husband did not come along, and it was just the four of us. When we got to the drive-in, she made her kids sit outside the car on a blanket to watch the movie, and we stayed in the car. She then invited me to sit next to her in the backseat. She said we should sit together in the middle of the seat so we could see the screen better though the middle of the front bucket seats. I clearly remember what movie we were watching because of what happened next. The movie was *The Godfather*. In one particular portion of the movie, the character Michael — who was the youngest son of gangster Don Corlione — kills two members of an opposing mob family and then flees to Sicily in hiding. While in Sicily he meets and falls in love with a beautiful young Sicilian girl. Through a series of events he ends up marrying her, and a provocative scene occurs on their wedding night. After entering their honeymoon suite, Michael closes the curtains to create an atmosphere of privacy, and as he turns to approach his new bride, she slowly lets her dress fall off her shoulders to expose her naked beauty to her new husband. It's a breathtaking scene, especially for a 14-year-old boy, let alone in the backseat of a car with a beautiful older woman. As this powerful scene was unfolding on the giant screen in front of us, the woman I was with warmly snuggled next to me, and quietly whispered in my ear, "Would you like it if I took off my shirt for you?" Although I remember these events as if they happened just yesterday, for the life of me I cannot remember what happened after that. I can't remember what I said or did, and I can't remember what she said or did. For some reason a thick fog surrounds the remainder of that night, as well as other incidents that occurred with this particular woman. What I do know and believe is that this woman also had a spirit of seduction and for whatever reasons, she chose to direct it toward me on numerous occasions.

My suspicion is that the spirit of seduction on these various women around me sensed my sexual weakness and vulnerability, and just like wolves can detect the slightest scent of blood, they were attracted to me accordingly. It's as though the enemy of my soul earned a right to access my sexuality through the gateway of generational sin[1] and the sinful bent of my own soul. As the soft underbelly of my vulnerability in this area was exposed, the enemy went out of his way to bring influences and other people into my life that would allow his grasp on me to progress from a toehold, to a grip, to a stronghold, and then to an addiction and bondage.

From studying the biblical principle of generational sin, we can surmise that parents with sexual issues may allow undo sexual vulnerability in the lives of their children. As in my case, my father's sexual weaknesses, demonstrated through his pornography and example of manhood, contributed and made me more vulnerable to the sexual weakness that was replicated in my life. Parents with issues of submission to authority and rebellion may allow such spirits to access and influence their children. Parents with issues of occultic practice or spiritism may allow such influences access to their children. The realization of these truths is very sobering, and especially scary for those of us who have children. As my sexual struggle continued, the fact that I had three sons often prompted me to continue the difficult path of healing and deliverance God had placed me on. I realized that not only was I fighting for the freedom of my own soul, but also for the freedom of my sons. This thought often compelled me to push ahead in the battle, even when I felt overwhelmed and hopeless. I desperately wanted God to heal the "hole" in my "umbrella," not only for my sake, but also for my boys.

---

1 The Bible teaches the principle of generational sin — see Exodus 20:5 and 34:7; Numbers 14:18; and Deuteronomy 5:9 — and says that the sins of the father will be visited upon the third and fourth generations of children. The truth of this principle can be illustrated as follows: imagine a father walking with his child through a rainstorm. As they walk together, the father holds an umbrella over the two of them, and the umbrella protects them both from the falling rain. But imagine what would happen if there was a big hole in one section of the umbrella. The rain would freely come through the hole and fall upon both the father and the child. In this illustration the umbrella represents the covering of God-given authority and protection a father has over his children. The rain represents the assault and attack of the devil upon our lives. When the father has an area of weakness, sin, or bondage in his own life, it's as though he has a hole in that area of spiritual authority and protection over his family. The devil is therefore able to access his life through this area — or hole — of weakness, and can thus also access the children through the same hole. If a man allows pornography and other wrong sexual influences in his life, it's as though he is opening a door that gives various spirits and demons the right to dwell with him. These might include spirits of lust, masturbation, and perversion. Since these spirits are allowed access, and more than that, have the right to exist in a particular home, they will now also have more direct access to the children's hearts in that home. As a result there is the very real possibility that the very areas of weakness, sin, and bondage that exist in parents will also be replicated in the lives of their children.

CHAPTER 6

DEEDS IN DARKNESS

There was a story in one of the magazines or books I read, I don't remember which, about an activity called pool hopping. The participants snuck around their neighborhood in the middle of the night under the cover of darkness, quietly slipped into their unsuspecting neighbors' swimming pools, took off their clothes to skinny-dip, and engaged in a variety of other activities. I was apparently taken with this idea because I decided to give it a try. Of course, there wasn't anyone else to participate, but I didn't let that small detail stop me.

In the middle of the night I snuck out and made my way to a neighbor's swimming pool. As I slipped into the water, I removed my bathing suit and began to move about the pool. As I did, I experienced one of the most arousing sensations of my young life. No doubt the combination of cool water flowing around my exposed body, the titillation of doing something forbidden, and the safety of the darkness that surrounded me all worked together to provide an unusual sense of erotic freedom. When I got out of the pool, I put my bathing suit back on and moved to another pool several houses away.

I recall doing this many different nights over a period of one summer, but one particular incident stands out in my mind. One night as I was getting out of a swimming pool, it occurred to me I didn't have to put my bathing suit back on as I moved to the next swimming pool. After all, it was completely dark, and I knew no one would be able to see me anyway. I there-

39

40 STORIES: THE REDEMPTION OF ONE MAN'S WOUNDED SEXUALITY

fore left my bathing suit off, and completely naked, I slipped through the neighborhood to the next pool. Adding this new ingredient to my wayward adventure must have contributed to my sense of excitement and exhilaration, and as I left the next pool, for some strange reason I began to run through the neighborhood. As I ran — completely naked — with the cool night air blowing against my wet skin, I felt a mysterious sense of freedom, and I ran faster and faster. As if someone had injected a mood-altering drug into my body, waves of exhilaration shot through me like electricity, empowering me to run faster and farther. As I approached one particular intersection, I suddenly saw beams of light in front of me and knew a car was fast approaching from a side street. I froze in my tracks, and realizing I was caught out in the open, I knew I didn't have time to hide before I would be seen. My only option was to quickly crouch behind a car that was parked near me on the street, and hope I wouldn't be noticed. As I peeked around the fender of the car that was hiding me, my heart leapt into my throat as I saw, of all things, a police car coming directly at me. I hugged the car as tightly as I could, and held my breath as the police car slowly passed just a few feet away. That experience was enough to scare the heck out of me, and as I quickly made my way back home, I knew my night pool adventures were over. It scares me even now to think about what would have happened if those policemen had seen me and caught me that night, and how I would have tried to explain what I was doing and why I was doing it.

Another time, my friend Kevin spent the night at my house. Kevin knew some girls from school who were having a sleepover, and had prearranged to call them at a certain time in the middle of the night. He said we were to contact the girls, and then sneak out to the house where they were. Since lust was raging in my heart like a forest fire — fueled by my exposure to pornography, masturbation, and the natural inclinations of my own sinful heart — I almost desperately wanted to get my hands on a real live girl. My secret desire was that I might be able to make out with one of these girls, or even participate in activities that, up to that time, I had only witnessed as a spectator of the books and magazines.

Knowing we couldn't use the phone at home because my parents might hear us, we decided to sneak out and walk to a nearby shopping plaza to use the payphone. Like real dummies, I guess it didn't occur to us that using a payphone in the middle of an asphalt field was like asking to get caught, and sure enough, as Kevin was talking on the phone, I saw a police car coming directly across the parking lot toward us. I instinctively yelled, "Cops!" as

Kevin dropped the phone, and we both began a mad dash for safety. He ran one way around the bank building in the parking lot, and I ran the other way. As I rounded the corner of the bank, I was confronted with the sprawling openness of the parking lot, and quickly realized I had nowhere to run. The safety of the backyards bordering the shopping center, and security of their shadows seemed like they were a million miles away, and I felt like I was trapped in the molasses of a bad dream as my legs seemed to move in slow motion. My mind raced faster than my body was moving as I desperately searched for a solution to my hopeless dilemma, and I quickly realized the closest place of sanctuary was a small ditch between the plaza's parking lot and entrance roadway. Since there was no other alternative, I made a bee-line in that direction and dove into the security of the shallow ditch.

As I peeked over the top edge of my new-found refuge, I saw the police car stopped and the ominous image of a policeman loading Kevin into the backseat. I pulled my head back down, and in a panic my mind continued to race as I tried to figure out what to do next. I knew I couldn't run for it. There was too much parking lot to cross, and I knew I would surely be seen. At the same time, I knew I couldn't stay in the ditch, because it was the only hiding spot around, and I knew it would be the first place the policeman would look in search of his quarry. As the computer of my mind hastily processed all available data in its vain attempt to find a solution, I was suddenly filled with terror when I saw the police car that had consumed Kevin coming directly toward me from across the parking lot. To make matters worse, I saw another police car with its lights flashing pulling into the shopping plaza, and my heart sank to the pit of my stomach as I realized there were now two "good" guys out there, and I was the "bad" guy they were pursuing.

With no other option, I slid as low as I could into the ditch, and hugged the ground as tight as I could. Suddenly, I saw the ditch explode with bright light about 50 yards away, and the bright beam of light began to slowly move down the ditch toward me as the policeman crept along the edge — his intense light piercing the safety of my hiding place. As the light approached closer and closer, in a final desperate attempt to conceal myself, I shut my eyes as tight as I could, but despite my final effort to disappear, I could suddenly feel myself engulfed by brilliant and penetrating light. Even with my eyes closed, I instantly felt completely exposed, and knew the whole world must be able to see me. Time seemed to stand still for several quiet moments, then, as if by magic, I was suddenly engulfed in darkness again. I opened my eyes in the dark, and as I turned my head to look in the opposite direction, I watched as the beam of light slowly continued moving down the ditch away from me.

Relief flooded over me as I realized in disbelief that the policeman hadn't seen me, and my heart raced at the hope that I might still be able to escape undetected. But, unfortunately, my joy was short lived as I suddenly heard a booming voice announce over the police loudspeaker, "Tony, come out! We know who you are! Tony, come out!" I couldn't believe my ears! With great disappointment I instantly knew my so-called friend, Kevin, had ratted me out. I hesitated for several moments as my mind desperately tried in vain to find a solution to my horrible dilemma, but quickly realized there was nothing I could do as the loudspeaker continued to boom my name for the world to hear, "Tony, come out! Tony, come out!" They obviously knew who I was, and even if I could somehow miraculously escape the parking lot, there was nowhere else to hide. All the cops had to do was show up at my house, and I knew they could get there before I could. With no other option, I slowly stood up and walked from the security of my hiding place to the exposure of the empty parking lot. The policeman, with his bright and blinding light piercing through my eyes to the depth of my soul, raced over to me and promptly hauled Kevin and I both to the police station for violation of curfew.

On the short ride to the police station, I sat in the front seat of the car, and the officer must have seen that I was completely terrorized because I remember him saying to me,

"It's not that big a deal, buddy. You're out after curfew, and we're just going to call your parents to come and get you."

I responded by saying, "Yeah, but you don't know my dad."

I knew I was in huge trouble — probably the worst trouble of my life — and that night did prove to be one of the worst nights of my life. I remember sitting on the couch in the family room when we got home, with my dad yelling at me, cussing me, and then hitting me. As his fury seemed to escalate, my mother attempted to rescue me as she tried in vain to stop him, and he suddenly and unfortunately turned his angry rage on her and started hitting her. It was one of the two times I know of that my father actually hit my mother, and as a result of the entire incident I was grounded to my room for a period of weeks.

About this same period of time, a young boy told me about a girl in our neighborhood who had oral sex with him. I was captured with this idea, and wondered if she would do the same thing to me. I'm sure my hormones were raging, and again, I was hungry to personally experience some of the many things I had read about so often. Sometime later I had the opportunity to be around this girl, and I asked her if she would do to me what she had done to the other boy. She said she would, and for this purpose I sought her out several different times in the weeks that followed. Although I was very young myself, this girl was several years younger than I was, and for this reason these incidents stand out as some of the most shameful memories of my past.

In recent years, through my own long and difficult healing process, which included extended periods of counseling, I slowly learned to grieve the violations and injustices that occurred against the innocence of my own youth, and I also learned to realize and grieve the ways in which I in turn violated others. I can't imagine the horror of this young girl's story, or what was going on in her life and home that brought her to the place where she would so easily engage in such activities with boys, and it deeply grieves me to this day to know that I contributed to her abuse and pain. I've often wondered about her. I've wondered where she is today and what her life is like. I've wondered how the early experiences of her childhood influenced her self image, the way she learned to relate to men, and her viewpoint of her own sexuality. I've wondered how she relates to men today, and how such things — if she ever got married — have affected her marriage. My basic understanding of sexual abuse is that it occurs when one person uses another for his or her own sexual pleasure without regard, concern, or understanding for how such activity might harm or influence that other person. As I learned of these things through my healing process, I realized to my own shame, that although I didn't understand the harm I was causing at the time, I sexually abused this young girl, and that knowledge saddens me deeply to this day.

Although this chapter reflects stories I would least want others to know, I feel they are important to convey because they represent what was happening in my own development and heart at the young ages of 14 and 15. Prior to this chapter, I shared primarily about who influenced the growth and development of my sexuality as a person, and how they did so. I talked more about what was done to me as opposed to what I myself did. I feel the stories conveyed in this chapter are important because they represent a kind of corner I was turning as my sexuality was adopting a life of its own, and I believe at this point I was already becoming deeply ensnared to a sexual addiction and bondage that would hold me captive for years to come. It's as if the earlier events of my life, through the various people and influences I've shared, were all sowing seed on the soil of my young heart, but at some point those seeds began to take root, grow, and bear fruit as they began to adopt lives of their own.

CHAPTER 7

Spiritual Awakening

Since I am Sicilian, I grew up Catholic, and my parents made me go to Religion School every Saturday, and to church every Sunday. When I was a kid, my mom said numerous times she wanted me to be a priest when I grew up, and I remember thinking to myself, "I can't even stand 1 hour of church, let alone going to church every day for the rest of my life." I have virtually no fond memories of this early religious training, and mostly remember how I couldn't wait for any given service in which I was involved to be over. One time I brought my papers home after a test in my religion class, and my mother laughed out loud when she reviewed the results. One question on the test asked what Jesus cried out when He was dying on the cross. My one-word answer was simply, "HELP!", which obviously proved I wasn't paying very good attention in class. The only other memory I have is watching a movie one Saturday night at church, sitting in the back row of the dark gymnasium with my friends, and pretending to vomit on the floor after mixing large mouthfuls of popcorn and orange soda.

Although I wasn't really interested in spiritual things when I was a child, and considered my involvement in church to be terribly boring, I did have a sincere belief that there really was a God, and I remember a couple of mysterious happenings that seemed to woo my heart toward the God I did not yet know. The first event involved my grandma, who was a deeply devout Catholic, and had mysterious tendencies toward premonitions. She told the

45

story many times of the last time she saw her niece, Catherine, before Catherine was killed in an automobile accident at the young age of 29. The entire family was together for dinner — a frequent occurrence in our Sicilian family — and after dinner Catherine approached my grandma to say good-bye. Grandma was seated, and as she turned and looked up at Catherine, she gasped and raised her hands in startled surprise. Catherine quickly inquired with alarm and concern, "What's wrong, Aunt Cecelia?" Grandma assured her everything was all right as she passed her sense of surprise off as nothing. It turned out to be the last time grandma saw Catherine alive, as Catherine was killed shortly afterward in a terrible automobile accident. It was only then grandma understood she had been given a sign from God, and reported the strange account of why she really reacted with surprise that evening. She explained that when she turned and looked at Catherine, her niece was surrounded with a bright light and appeared to have a kind of halo around her head. That's why grandma gasped. From that time forward grandma always believed that God had given her this sign indicating Catherine's impending death. As grandma later told this story at different times as I was growing up, I remember a sense of curiosity stirring deep in my heart, and I somehow knew there must be a real God to allow my grandma to see such visions.

Strangely, the other event that wooed my heart and confirmed the reality of the spirit world also involved an automobile accident and a death at the age of 29. My father's best friend was a young man named Bob, and Bob was tragically killed in this accident. He left behind a young widow named Donna and two small children, one of whom was only a couple months old at the time. Bob was killed late at night, and after receiving the terrible news, my father was going to visit Donna and pay his respects the next day. My father invited me to go along with him, and as we drove the lengthy distance to where Donna lived, we rode in mournful silence. After a considerable visit, we said good-bye and headed back home. Along the way we came to a particular intersection, and as we sat waiting for the red light to change, my father broke the silence by pointing out our location. We were stopped next to the mortuary where Bob's body was being prepared for burial, and where we would be returning the next day to attend the funeral. My father simply said, "Tony, that's where Bob is right now. His body is in that funeral home." The irony appeared when we arrived home, and my father pointed out that on our entire journey to and from Donna's house, which was a considerable distance across the city of St. Louis, every single stoplight we crossed was green except for one: the one red light we encountered at the very corner where Bob's body was. I was stunned by this event, and although I didn't have any idea what it meant, I knew again, deep in my heart, that there must be a God to allow such a strange and unexplained thing to happen. I knew what happened couldn't just be a coincidence. Years later I came to believe that God allowed these special occurrences in order to bring glimpses of light into my dark soul and to begin preparing my heart for the seed of the gospel.

Later, when I was 16 years old, I was invited to a non-denominational Bible study for young people. I heard there would be a lot of pretty girls there, and probably attended more for that reason in the beginning than any other. What I found was a lively group of young people who were sincerely and seriously interested in spiritual things, and as I attended the various social events and weekly meetings, I began to genuinely consider the message of the Bible for the first time in my life. Although I had attended church for years, I had never read the Bible. As I began to comprehend its message for the first time, I felt familiar and mysterious stirrings in my heart and was reminded of my Grandma's stories and the mystery of the red light. I could feel myself being drawn to understand more, and like the dawning of a new day slowly chases away darkness as the sun peeks over the distant horizon, the eyes of my spiritual understanding were slowly being opened. I had always heard with my head that God loved me, but it seemed I was now beginning to hear with my heart.

I had grown up with the image of God as an angry old man in heaven who was displeased with me and looking for reasons to punish me. I thought it was up to me to somehow appease this angry God by going to church and doing other good deeds that would somehow make Him happy. I always pictured God and His judgment like a big teeter-totter in the sky. I imagined every time I did something bad, God put it on one side of the teeter-totter, and every time I did something good, He put it on the other side. I thought it was up to me to create enough good deeds in my life to somehow offset my bad deeds in an attempt to make myself acceptable to this angry God who was keeping score. I was therefore stunned when I began to study the Bible and learned that my entire image of God was completely wrong.

I learned that no matter how hard I tried I could never take away my own sins — that I could never create enough good deeds to offset my bad deeds (Ephesians 2:8–9; Romans 4:5; Galatians 2:16, 21; Titus 3:5). I learned that Jesus Christ had died on the cross to make a complete payment for all my sins, that he had risen from the dead 3 days later, and that having a true relationship with God and eternal life was a gift God offered me freely based upon what Jesus had done for me (I Corinthians 15:3–4; Romans 6:23). I learned the only thing I could do to become a child of God was to simply believe in, by faith, what Jesus had done for me, and ask Jesus to be my Savior (John 1:12, 3:16, and 6:47; I John 5:13). As I began to understand these things, I prayed a simple prayer, and although I don't remember the exact words I said, my prayer went something like this:

> Dear God, I know that I am a sinner. I know I cannot take away my own sins. I understand that Jesus died on the cross to take away my sins, and He came back from the dead 3 days later. I ask Jesus to do for me what I cannot do for myself. I ask Jesus to come into my heart, to be my Savior, to take away my sins, to make me His child, and to take me to heaven when I die.

Although I did not fully understand everything that happened to me the moment I prayed this little prayer, as I continued to grow in my faith and study the Bible, I came to believe that the moment I prayed that prayer was the most important moment of my life. I learned that in that moment everything in my life was changed. I had passed from death unto life. My eternal destiny changed from hell to heaven. The angels in heaven were rejoicing over my salvation. All the sins I had ever committed — or ever would commit — had been paid for by the death of Jesus on the cross, and they no longer separated me from my heavenly father. God was in my life, and the Holy Spirit actually came to dwell within my heart. I entered a personal and intimate relationship with the God of the universe at that very moment — a relationship that made Him my father, and made me His child. And although I was not miraculously healed or delivered from the person I was or the bent in my soul toward sexual addiction and bondage, I had inherited a completely new foundation to my life. God was in my life now, and just as He delivered me from the penalty of my sins to bring Jesus into my life through justification, He would begin to deliver me from the power of sin in order to make me more like Jesus every day through sanctification. Although it would be a profoundly messy and painful process, God now slowly could begin to change my life from the inside out, as you'll see in the pages ahead.

CHAPTER 8

My First Girlfriend, the Tasmanian Devil, & the Cycle

Shortly after I began attending the Bible study, a particular young lady also began to attend. I was immediately enchanted with her, and was delighted when she seemed interested in me. One day she called me and asked if we could talk. She was crying and was obviously very upset. We made arrangements and met a short time later at a local restaurant. There she shared with me a secret that only a couple of her closest friends knew. She told me she had been dating this guy, and she had sex with him the week before. She said it was the first time she had ever had sex, and she was scared to death she might be pregnant. I'm sure that as a 16-year old I was completely ill-prepared to offer her any kind of appropriate advice. I think I primarily listened and then encouraged her to wait and see what happened. Mostly, I felt completely flattered that she trusted me with her secret, and I'm sure that both her willingness to share such an intimate thing with me, and my willingness to listen, went a long way toward drawing us closer and creating a kind of bond between us. After that, we started spending more time together, and I quickly fell head over heels in love with her.

49

I remember the first time we kissed. We were alone in the basement of her parents' house, and as we sat on the couch, we began kissing. As we continued to do so for some extended period of time, she took my hand and moved it toward an area of her body I knew as a Christian I wasn't supposed to touch. I resisted her invitation and told her I didn't think we should do that. She responded by pulling my hand even harder, and as I continued to resist her advance, she finally surrendered, gave me a tight hug, and thanked me for being so "strong." In retrospect, and for reasons you'll see as my story continues to unfold, I believe this young lady was also over-sexualized and had a spirit of seduction about her.

After we first kissed, like two powerful magnets irresistibly drawn toward one another, we continued to do so every time we were together. It seemed as though each episode was more intimate than the previous, and in a short matter of time we were doing things we should not have been doing. As the level of passion between us grew, so did our physical involvement with one another, and as we yielded to this natural progression, we quickly arrived at the final destination of sexual intercourse. Although I clearly remember the first time it happened, I'll not share details about the event itself. Instead, I'd rather share what happened immediately afterward, because I think it represents a kind of cycle I would become trapped in for years to come. As we sat in the dark next to each other, a strange dichotomy swirled through my soul, as if I was both Dr. Jeckyl and Mr. Hyde. Part of me felt a sense of guilt and shame, because I knew I should not have done what I had just done. But another part of me was thrilled, and I remember thinking to myself with a kind of delight, "I can't believe it. I just had sex. I'm not a virgin anymore. I can't believe it." As we sat there, surrounded by darkness, my thoughts were quickly interrupted when I realized she was quietly crying. She said she felt bad and she was afraid she might be pregnant. I did my best to comfort her, and as we talked I remember telling her three different things. I told her God understood our weakness, that He would forgive us, and that we would never do it again. Then we actually prayed together, and when I prayed I mentioned all three of these things in my prayer to God.

In retrospect I believe my immediate response to my failure — God understands, God will forgive me, and I'll never do it again — was significant, because it marked the beginning of a cycle that defined my struggle to control my sexuality for years to come. In the same way water finds a small crack in a hill during a rain and follows the crack downhill, carving it over time from a crack, to a rivulet, to a gully, and then to a ditch — I found

My First Girlfriend, the Tasmanian Devil, & the Cycle 51

myself returning over and over again, whenever I failed, to the same series of thoughts I had on the first night I had sex — God understands, God will forgive me, and I'll never do it again. That basic cycle usually started with me expressing my sexuality in a way I knew was displeasing to God — like lusting in my mind, having premarital sex, or committing adultery. I almost immediately felt some level— from mild to severe — of shame, guilt, and conviction. It was then I would remember and hope that God understood my weakness. I normally prayed and asked God to forgive me, and then I sincerely promised God that I would never do it again. On the mere strength of this promise and my genuine desire to do the right thing, I typically lasted anywhere from several days to several weeks before my archenemy showed up, causing me to fail again, and then the cycle would start all over.

This enemy, which I later referred to figuratively as the Tasmanian Devil for lack of a better name, represented the overwhelming and powerful sexual desire that lived within me and constantly demanded my obedience. I pictured him as a fierce, incredibly powerful little monster with hypnotic beady eyes, sharp claws, and razor-like fangs. It was me against him, and although I did my best to resist him whenever he showed up — which was pretty often — he inevitably got the best of me. I normally had the strength to hold him off for a period of time. It's as if when he showed up I could restrain him by forcing him into a trashcan, putting the lid on it, and then sitting on top of it using my weight in the attempt to keep him caged. But he was very strong, and as he continuously banged, kicked, and clawed in rebellion to the internment I subjected him to, my strength eventually faded, and despite my valiant efforts against him, he would burst out of my fragile confine, leap on top of me, sink his fangs and claws deep into my flesh, and defeat me once again. Of course, it wasn't really me against him, as if there were two personalities struggling against one another. In reality the Tasmanian Devil had a name, and his name was Tony.

CHAPTER 9
My Pastor & My Girlfriend

My girlfriend and I continued to date — and to be sexually active — through my senior year in high school. Although I struggled deeply with controlling my sexuality, I loved the Lord and wanted to spend my life serving Him, so I decided to go to Bible college after high school graduation. I was attending a young church at the time that had grown out of the youth ministry I was involved with, and I deeply loved my pastor. It was through his ministry and influence that I had become a Christian, and since I loved and respected him so much, upon his recommendation, I decided to attend the same Bible college that he had graduated from. Several other kids I knew from our youth group were already attending the college, and I determined to join their rank the following Fall. My girlfriend also decided to attend the same Bible college, and although we had graduated from high school at the same time, she decided she wasn't going to start college until second semester, which meant we would be apart for about 4 months. So through a difficult series of events, which included leaving my girlfriend and being disowned by my father because of my decision to go to Bible college, I put everything I owned in a cardboard box, and with $50.00 in my pocket I set out for my future. Although it was difficult being apart, and although I missed her terribly, I stayed in almost constant touch with my girlfriend and anticipated our reunion at the end of the semester. I couldn't wait to get home and see her, and I couldn't wait for her to join me at college the next semester.

When I returned home for Christmas break, I immediately called my girlfriend and we made arrangements to meet that evening. I was so happy to see her, and after exchanging gifts, we sat next to each other in a darkened family room, lit only by the soft and shimmering light of the Christmas tree. As we talked for some period of time, she seemed oddly distant, and I could tell something was troubling her. In response to my gentle coaxing she said she didn't want to tell me what was bothering her because she didn't want to hurt me, and she didn't want to ruin someone's ministry. Completely confused, I continued to question her, and she finally confessed to me that since I had been gone, she had been having an affair with — of all people — our pastor! She said it had been going on for several months, and they had been sexually active. As she spoke she began to cry. She told me she knew it was wrong. She said she loved me. She said she wanted me to forgive her and she wanted to be with me. She said she didn't want to ruin his ministry or cause the new church to end. She said she wanted to end her affair with our pastor, and she wanted to go away with me to Bible college. I remember comforting her and telling her that I loved her too. I told her that I wanted to be with her if she wanted to be with me, and I told her that I forgave her. We then prayed together, and as we talked afterward, she told me she would end her affair with our pastor the next night at the church Christmas party.

When we arrived at the party the next night, our pastor's house was crowded. It was good to see my friends, and I kept busy with many conversations. But mostly I remember feeling awkward around my pastor, and nervous about the talk I knew my girlfriend was going to have with him. A short time later, I saw the two of them slip out the back door, and I remember praying that God would help her find the right words to say and the courage to say them. They were gone for some extended period of time, and I felt a great sense of relief when they finally returned. I couldn't wait to hear what happened, and on the way home I asked her to tell me what had occurred. Although I don't remember her exact words, she conveyed that she had ended the affair. I remember feeling relieved, and then with a kind of insecure jealousy, I asked her if anything had happened between them. She told me she would rather not say because she didn't want to hurt me. It was obvious from her words that something had happened, and when I insisted upon knowing, she told me they had held hands as they talked, and they kissed good-bye. I remember feeling hurt and confused by her confession, and when I inquired further she told me that he wanted to kiss her one last time, and that he had made the kiss happen. Although I didn't like the fact that she had allowed him to kiss her, I knew she would be leaving in a couple days with me for college. I trusted her promise to me that it was over, and I knew the twelve hundred miles that would separate them would prevent anything further from happening — or so I thought.

Since my girlfriend had ended the affair, and since she was going back to Bible college with me, I didn't think it necessary to confront my pastor about what had happened, and I didn't say a word to him about it. Years later, as part of my own counseling process, my therapist thought this part of my story was very strange, and wanted to explore it further. He was intrigued by my complete absence of anger and outrage toward my pastor because of what had happened, and further intrigued by my unwillingness to face him. Over a period of numerous counseling sessions, as we explored my lack of reaction to the affair, at one point my counselor actually asked me if anything physical had happened between my pastor and I. When I realized what he was suggesting, I was shocked. He was asking me if any homosexual interactions had ever occurred between the two of us. I assured him that nothing like that had ever happened, and asked him why he would even suggest such a thing. He said that such a scenario could explain the unusual level of loyalty and confidence I displayed toward my pastor, in spite of his betrayal of me. Why else would I respond in such an understanding and forgiving manner to a situation that should have completely outraged me? As we talked further — over a period of several weeks — a kind of picture began to emerge, and I began to understand my strange lack of emotion so many years ago.

It was a picture of me as a young boy who was lacking an appropriate relationship with a dominant male figure. As a young boy, I did not have a very healthy relationship with my own father. My father was angry and distant most of the time, and there was a lack of an emotional connection between the two of us. There was virtually no affection between us, and my father never touched me, except in anger. The primary feeling I had toward my father was fear, and with this kind of emotional void in my life, I was apparently almost desperate for a healthy relationship with an older male — someone I could look up to and trust; someone who would touch me and hug me in a healthy and loving way. I needed someone who would talk with me, spend time with me, recognize me, affirm me, and make me feel important. Then, at the age of 16, I finally met the older male role model I didn't even know I was searching for, and he happened to be my pastor. He became my friend, and I quickly grew to love and respect him. I wanted to emulate him, and I wanted him to approve of me and be proud of me. I felt a kind of emotional connection and warmth between the two of us, and in a strange way I came to the place where I needed our relationship — so much so, that when my pastor did something that deeply violated our relationship, I was apparently willing to look the other way. Only after many years passed and after many difficult counseling sessions would I slowly begin to find the appropriate feelings toward my pastor and the situation that had happened so many years ago — feelings of pain and anger, outrage and tears.

CHAPTER 10

My Pastor
& "Thou Art
the Man"

After Christmas break, I left St. Louis and the awkward situation with my pastor and returned to Bible college with my girlfriend. Since I knew what had happened between them, I felt relieved that they were now separated, and naively thought that their affair was over. Since she had broken off the relationship with him, and they were now separated by over twelve hundred miles, and since she had promised me that she wanted to be with me, I thought the whole messy situation was now behind us, and that everything would be all right. I guess I trusted that he would come to his senses, continue serving the Lord, and that would be the end of that.

Imagine therefore, my surprise when my girlfriend told me she was receiving love letters from him in the mail! They were always anonymous letters, with no return address, and they were signed in a generic fashion such as, "From You Know Who." She would show me the letters, and we were both shocked that he was writing the things that he was writing. Although I remember various things he wrote, I think it best not to mention any specifics. His words were certainly risqué and completely inappropriate for a married man — let alone a pastor — to be writing to a teenage girl. The letters made it obvious that he was not letting the matter die, and the affair was

57

58   STORIES: THE REDEMPTION OF ONE MAN'S WOUNDED SEXUALITY

at least continuing to rage in his heart. Although I had no idea what to do about this new development, I at least felt protected by the distance between us, and hoped our time apart would allow the situation to settle down. Imagine the panic I felt, therefore, when I heard our pastor was coming to visit!

Every year the Bible college we attended had a missions conference. Various alumni, missionaries, and speakers came from all around the country and from foreign lands for a kind of grand reunion and celebration. Although he had never attended the mission conference previously, our pastor sent word that he would be coming for the conference that year, and said he would be coming alone since his wife was unable to attend. Of course, I knew in my heart he wasn't really coming for the mission conference at all. It was simply a convenient excuse for him to visit, and in reality he was coming to continue his pursuit of my girlfriend. It was at that point I knew I had no other choice: I would have to confront him about the situation. As the days leading up to his visit slowly ticked by, I quietly dreaded the day of his arrival. I prayed and asked God to not let him come, and I prayed that if he did come God would help me to speak the right words to him. As a young teenager who had only been a Christian for just over a year, I was not looking forward to the responsibility of confronting the man I loved and considered my mentor. I remembered the story of when the prophet Nathan confronted David regarding his sin with Bathsheba, and I struggled deeply as I contemplated how I would say the words to my pastor, "Thou art the man."

The dreaded day arrived, and my girlfriend told me that our pastor had asked her — immediately upon his arrival — if they could meet later that evening. I knew I couldn't allow that meeting to take place, so with much trepidation I approached my pastor and told him I needed to talk with him. I could tell he was immediately nervous, and was surely suspicious of my motive. We agreed to take a walk behind the college along the beach of the beautiful Atlantic Ocean, and as we walked I told him I knew what had happened between him and my girlfriend. He asked me what I knew, and I told him I knew everything. I told him I knew about the affair, and I told him I knew they had been sexually involved. Although I don't remember a lot about our discussion, I do recall a couple specific things. Among them I remember sharing a silly illustration with him concerning an old shoe and a hammer. Using this illustration, I told my pastor that if someone needs to hammer a nail in the wall, it would be best to use a hammer. But if a hammer is not available the person could instead use the heel of an old shoe to bang the nail in the wall. I told him I wanted him to be a hammer in God's hand instead of an old shoe, so God could use him more effectively in ministry. I also told him I loved him, and that I didn't want to see him lose his family or his ministry.

Another thing I recall is his response to our discussion. He told me the real reason he had come to visit was to end the affair with my girlfriend. He implied that she was the one who was trying to keep it alive, but he knew it was completely wrong, and he had come to break it off with her once and for all. I was suspicious of his words, and felt in my heart that he was lying. I knew of the letters that he had been sending her, and felt that he had come to continue his pursuit of her. I didn't have the strength, know-how, or courage to confront his dishonest words, but I discerned in my heart that I really didn't need to. I sensed that my confronting him was in a sense like throwing a bucket of ice water in his face, and knew that our discussion would bring the affair to a grinding halt. Despite what I believed to be his dishonesty about why he came to visit that week, I was satisfied that the affair would finally be officially over, so I didn't feel compelled to push past his words into his heart's true motives. I remember him asking me if anyone else knew about it, and I assured him I hadn't told anyone. He asked me if I would be willing to protect him and the church by keeping the matter quiet. He then promised me that he had learned some hard lessons, and that he would never allow such a thing to happen again. I gave him my promise, and in a strange way felt privileged that we now shared such an intimate secret.

In retrospect, as I remember and contemplate these events, I'm amazed at how unhealthy and dysfunctional I must have been. I wonder, "Who was that young man, and what was he thinking?" I wonder why I wasn't deeply offended by the actions of both my girlfriend and my pastor. I wonder why I was so willing to understand, forgive, and look the other way. I wonder why I was willing to keep my pastor's secret, and how the future might have been different had I chosen another path. Because of my silence over the years regarding this matter, many things happened on different fronts as life continued to unfold. My pastor remained in the ministry and his young church continued to grow. It would be years later before the truth eventually surfaced that he had been sexually involved with several other women in the church. Several of the kids who had gone away to Bible college eventually graduated, came back to St. Louis, and worked with the church.

Eventually, the mother church headed by my pastor grew and resulted in three other sister-church spin-offs. I sometimes thought that it was because of my silence that these four churches even existed, because if I would have blown the whistle on my pastor, he would have lost his ministry, the first church would have ended, and none of the other churches would have even existed.

But mostly I wonder how my own future might have changed if my pastor's sin had been properly dealt with so many years ago. Because of how things unfolded at the time, I believe his example deeply impacted my own life in a very harmful way. Just as my physical father taught me about sexuality and women through his life and example, I believe my pastor — as my spiritual father — also taught me through his life and example. He was teaching me that it was all right to be a man of God and to fail sexually; that such a man could remain in ministry. His life and example reaffirmed many of the wrong messages I had learned as a child from my father. My pastor taught me that there really isn't that big of a difference between how a common man — like my father — and a man in the ministry handles his sexuality and relates to women. It's almost as though — unbeknownst to me — my pastor's example gave me permission to fail sexually. In the years that followed, as I continued to struggle deeply with controlling my own sexuality, and as I failed repeatedly, I frequently thought to myself, "I know I shouldn't fail like this, but God understands. It's hard to be a man. After all, even my pastor struggled with this just like I do, and he remained in the ministry and God continued to use him. Even King David failed sexually, but God allowed him to continue being King. God, I know that you understand my weakness. Please forgive me, and I promise I will try to never do it again." Thus, the behavior of both my father and my pastor created a tag-team effect that exerted a powerful and horrible influence on the development of my own sexuality.

Chapter 11
The Golden Boy

My girlfriend and I stayed together through the end of my junior year in college. At that point we had been together for over 4 years, and although it's hard for me to remember exactly why, we mutually decided to break up. Since it was the only relationship either one of us had ever had, and given the familiarity of being together for so long, I think we were both interested and curious about the possibility of dating other people. We agreed to separate for a time and date other people, and agreed that we could always get back together if we discovered we were meant for one another. That meant I was a free agent and would be able to date anyone I wanted to — assuming the feelings were mutual — and since I was elected student body president for my upcoming senior year in college, I was looking forward to the opportunity. There were many beautiful young women among the student population of over one thousand, and I sensed the prestige of my position as student body president would provide unlimited opportunities.

Of course, this new-found freedom also brought with it a kind of dilemma. While I was excited about the prospect of dating other girls, I knew in my heart there was the ever-present danger of the Tasmanian Devil. Given my highly visible position as student body president, I knew there would be many people watching me and expecting a lot from me in terms of both the leadership and example that I would provide. I was determined to do my best and uphold the confidence my peers had placed in me. So with more resolve than ever, starting the summer of my senior year, I pushed the Tasmanian Devil into his trashcan and after searching my soul's inventory, put my heaviest lock on the lid. Of course, my determination to assert authority over the power of my sexualized soul was a mere illusion of self-control. In reality, the fruit that is always born is consistent with the nature that lives within, and it didn't take long for the determination of my self-will to be humbled once again. As I continued to fight the reality of the person I was on the inside, my efforts proved as vain as a dog who decides he will never bark or wag his tail again, or an apple tree that decides to no longer bear apples.

Like steam rising and quickly vanishing from a boiling pot of water — whenever I was confronted with the opportunity to be intimate with a member of the opposite sex — my determination quickly evaporated. It seemed as though I simply didn't have the strength of character to make myself do the right thing. This led to a couple different sexual encounters during the summer break before my senior year of college, including a whirlwind weekend liaison with a young lady I met at a friend's wedding, and an entanglement with a divorced woman. Since both of these situations had occurred far away from the college I was attending, I felt a kind of safety in the distance that separated them from the stage I would soon be on at school.

When I returned to college, I knew I had to clean up my act or risk certain exposure if I failed again in the close confines of a college environment. As it happened, I didn't even date anyone my senior year of college. I had been granted a full-tuition scholarship as student body president, and my hectic schedule spent fulfilling my duties kept me very busy most of the time. Added to that was my almost natural reluctance because of the tabloid-like gossip that would surely surround my dating activity, and of course, there was always my underlying fear that the Tasmanian Devil might escape if given the opportunity.

As a result of these influences, I was able to stay out of trouble sexually for my entire senior year...almost. As the end of the school year approached, along with my graduation and ordination into the ministry, I had the opportunity to go on a weekend trip with several other students. We were to stay at a couple of different homes while visiting with one particular family and church for the weekend. Also on this trip was one particular young lady who I knew had been infatuated with me for the entire year. Although she was attractive in several ways, I was in no way interested in her, primarily because she had rather obvious scars on her face and a speech impediment as the result of a birth defect. Although I frequently sensed the "vibe" from her throughout the year, I was careful to avoid her, and was not seriously tempted by her because I was not attracted to her. As things worked out that particular weekend, we spent considerable time alone together, and as one thing led to another, we ended up having sexual intercourse. I remember telling her beforehand that I was not interested in having a relationship with her, and I wanted to make sure she understood that. She said she knew we wouldn't be together, but that she still wanted to have sex with me. We ended up doing so, and then had sex at least two other times that I remember after we returned to school. It was the very end of the school year, and it seemed as though the Tasmanian Devil erupted with a vengeance after being caged for so many months. I only hoped that since the end of the year was so close my failure would be undetected.

I consider this particular relationship to be one of the most shameful things in my life, for several reasons. I was student body president that year. I had been entrusted with the stewardship and responsibility of leadership. People were counting on me to uphold the integrity of my office, and I had obviously failed. Although I was a gifted leader and speaker outwardly, the people around me had no idea how deeply my soul was in bondage to the lesser god of my sexuality.

I used this particular girl in such a terrible way for my own sexual gratification, further confirming my status as a sexual abuser. I had told her I wasn't interested in a relationship with her, but I was willing to take her body and use it for selfish gratification when she offered it to me. I'm especially ashamed of the fact that although we had sex several times, I only kissed her once that I remember. I didn't want to kiss her because of the scars on her face, yet I was willing to use her body sexually. It deeply saddens me to think of how this must have impacted her, and the message it must have sent to her regarding the confirmation of her self-image. And then, possibly most shameful of all, is the fact that I had sex with her on the very night of my ordination. I was, in a sense, the golden boy of my Bible college that year. I was elected as the leader of the entire school from a student body of over one thousand. I conducted meetings, oversaw events, and preached sermons. I had been elected and approved through an extensive ordination process, and yet, within mere hours of my ordination as a minister of Jesus Christ, I had premarital sexual intercourse with a girl I didn't even care about. I had all the outer appearances of success, but no one knew of my deep inner personal bondage — at least not yet.

Chapter 12

Canaan

After graduating from Bible college, I returned to St. Louis. I had no intention of staying there permanently, as I was considering a couple of different ministry opportunities around the country. Since I didn't have clear direction, I thought I would go home for the summer and see where the Lord would lead me from there. I didn't really feel welcome in St. Louis in terms of ministry, primarily because of the situation involving my pastor and my ex-girlfriend. Whenever I was around him, such as when I was at home visiting during various school breaks, I felt that he was uncomfortable with my presence and wished I wasn't even around. I knew about his moral failure, and he knew that I knew, and I believe that made him uncomfortable with me. In fact, I felt many times that he was even patronizing me. It seemed as though he would go out of his way to be extra nice to me, and I frequently felt suspicious of his motives.

In addition to my suspicions regarding my pastor's motives toward me, there was another indicator of his heart toward me through an obvious sign of omission on his part. He did not invite me to come back and be part of the ministry in St. Louis. A couple other young men from our church had graduated from the same Bible college, and they had been given invitations to come back to St. Louis to work with the church. A foundational principle of the church's vision was to expand God's kingdom through church planting, and the church had a preliminary plan to groom young leaders specifically for the purpose of launching new churches in the St. Louis area. These other young men were invited to be a part of this exciting vision, and had already been incorporated as part of the church leadership team. It seemed logical and obvious that I would be the next candidate in the furtherance of this vision, but rather than being invited to consider and pray

66   STORIES: THE REDEMPTION OF ONE MAN'S WOUNDED SEXUALITY

about such an opportunity, no such invitation was ever extended to me. In fact, I remember having one conversation with my pastor where he clearly encouraged me to seek ministry opportunities elsewhere around the country. It seemed obvious that he didn't want me around, so I was praying and waiting for the Lord to show me where I was supposed to go.

As the days began to pass that summer, I met a group of three teenage boys who often played music and hung out in my neighbor's basement. They had a jam session almost every day, and since I had recently acquired a guitar and wanted to learn how to play, I asked them if I could join them. Of course, I was looking for opportunities to have a ministry in the lives of people, and thought these boys would make a fine mission field while I was at home. As it turned out, all three of these boys were raised in Christian homes, but they were all somewhat disenchanted with the religiosity of their parents' churches, and none of them were seriously interested in spiritual things. As we began to make music together, I began to share with them and challenge them spiritually, and I began to have a kind of discipleship ministry in their lives. We got together for our jam sessions almost every day, and then we had Bible studies where I shared various lessons with them. There were several other teenagers in the neighborhood, friends of these boys along with others, and soon several of them began sitting in on our jam sessions and Bible studies. As friends invited friends to the gathering, there was soon a basement full of kids attending, and it seemed as if my own youth ministry had spontaneously erupted. We even had a built-in worship team since we had been practicing our music for many weeks.

Of course, I had just graduated from Bible college, and I had been taught for the last 4 years to go out and win the world for Christ. That, coupled with my natural gifts as a leader and motivator, and my own less-than-pure ambition to do great things for God, made it easy for me to believe that God wanted me to start my own ministry and was directing me to do so through the natural progression of these events. As more kids began attending our meetings, I saw it as confirmation of God's will and hand of blessing. As I thought I was waiting in St. Louis for God to show me what I should do, it seemed as though He showed me His will by dumping a ministry right in my lap. In hindsight, while I believe God used my sincere efforts of serving Him to impact the lives of many people, I eventually realized that — because of the moral weakness that still lived within me — I was in fact completely ill-prepared for the responsibilities of ministry.

When the ministry first started, we had a weekly meeting on Tuesday nights. We soon added a Friday-night fellowship that included some sort of social activity and just hanging out. The only thing that was missing was church on Sunday morning. As more kids came to Christ, I knew it was important to get them involved in a church, and I began bringing a couple of carloads of kids — mostly those who had never been to church before — to my pastor's church. It was the only church I was personally acquainted with, and my circle of Christian friends all went to church there, so I didn't really know where else to take these kids. The only problem was the issue between my pastor and I, which was an issue that seemed to loom large between us. I felt that he didn't want me around, so somewhere along the line I began having discussions with a number of our group about the possibility of starting our own church. Several people had been asking me to start a meeting on Sunday morning, and I didn't need very much encouragement to begin moving in that direction.

Since this new church would be across town, I knew I would have to talk with my pastor about my decision. I remember a series of events that culminated in a meeting with the leadership of my pastor's church. There were basically four main leaders — including my pastor — of the church at the time, and as we discussed the possibility of my new church, each member of the council was given the opportunity to share his thoughts. In the end, one person was in favor of me beginning the church, two were neutral — including my pastor — and one was opposed. In the face of such an inconclusive opinion, they basically determined that it was up to me to do whatever I felt God was leading me to do, and so I made the decision that I would start a new church.

In retrospect, I believe this process is another way in which my pastor deeply failed me. He was the senior leader among the group, and the man I most respected and wanted to emulate at the time. Although he wasn't privy to any of the details, I believe he was at least suspicious of my sexual weakness, and certainly knew it was premature for me to be in any leadership capacity as serious as pastoring a new church. I believe that in his heart he knew I shouldn't do such a thing, but was afraid to express his true feelings because of his own need for self-preservation. How could he express to me that I wasn't prepared for ministry, when I knew that he had already blown it in his ministry? He must have sensed that such a stand toward me would have constituted a serious level of hypocrisy on his behalf, thus because of his uncomfortable feelings toward me, he took the path of least resistance.

After several discussions, the new ministry and the church was named

Canaan. The idea was that in the Bible, God's promised land, Canaan, was a place flowing with milk and honey, and the place of God's blessing and provision. Little did I know or understand how appropriate the name would turn out to be, because on the way to Canaan, God's people fell into sin, and were then required to wander in the wilderness for another 40 years.

Chapter 13

Public Shame

There's no way Tony can continue to be our pastor. What he has done is wrong, and he has an obvious problem in his life that he has to deal with. By his actions he has hurt not only those he has been involved with, but he has also hurt our church, and ultimately the kingdom of God. I still love Tony and appreciate all he has done, but my conscience requires me to cast my vote against him. It's time for him to step aside.

The words of my trusted friend pierced my heart like an arrow, but I couldn't hate him for what he said because I knew he spoke the truth. It was the most difficult day of my life — to that point — as our entire church convened for a kind of public hearing to vote on whether I should continue to be their pastor. The church was almost 2 years old, and my continued sexual sin had finally become public knowledge. As word of my indiscretions spread like a giant game of dominoes from person to person through the church, it became clear the cat was out of the bag regarding my sexual weakness.

In what I now believe was another significant error to add to my already long list of mistakes, including my many sexual failures, the lack of wisdom I displayed by believing I could be in the ministry despite my obvious Achilles' heel, and my arrogance in believing I was ready at such a young age to assume the significant responsibilities of starting and pastoring a church — I allowed those around me to conduct two public hearings in order to determine my fate along with that of the new church. It would be years later before I would come to clearly see that I should have never allowed those meetings to occur. The more honorable thing for me to do, recognizing my clear disqualification for ministry, would have been to immediately resign as pastor of the church, saving its members the further pain and ill-will that surely would have resulted from the opposing viewpoints expressed in such meetings. Instead, the church decided to hold two public meetings to allow its members to determine through a vote whether I should remain their pastor. Three distinct segments would characterize the meetings. First, I would be given the opportunity to make a statement of confession, repentance, and apology for my transgressions. Then the floor would be open to anyone who wanted to speak, either for or against me, and finally a vote would be taken allowing each member's voice to be heard through his or her ballot. Each member was to vote simply "yes" or "no" indicating if I should continue to be pastor, and it was agreed that a simple majority would determine the outcome. The meetings were to be officiated with the help of a leader from none other than my pastor's church, and for obvious reasons, my pastor sent one of his co-leaders to handle the responsibility. No doubt it would have been very awkward for him to conduct a tribunal judging my sexual failures when he himself was guilty of the same charge.

For an event in my life I have wished many times I could forget, there are multiple things about the meetings I still remember, even now as I write these words some 20 years later. I remember making my public confession. I read from Psalm 51, which is David's Psalm of confession and contrition after his adulterous affair with Bathsheba. I admitted that I had sexual intercourse with one young lady in the church, and that I had been inappropriately involved with two other girls. I said I was sorry for what I had done wrong, that I was sorry for any harm or pain I had caused the girls I had been involved with, that I had learned a hard lesson, that I would do my best to honor God in the future if I was allowed to remain pastor, and I asked for forgiveness. Although I believe the words I offered were sincere, I also know in hindsight that my confession was far from complete. I know now that I minimized my sin by admitting only to the transgressions for which I had already been caught. I said nothing of another young lady I had also had sex with numerous times that no one knew about, and I said nothing of my past or the reality of my deep struggle to control my sexuality for so many years.

Like the tip of a dangerous iceberg, the people around me were seeing only a small part of a problem in my life that was really much bigger and hidden under the surface. Of course, at this time I myself didn't even comprehend the enormity of my problem. I tended to minimize my failures as things I did wrong on the outside as opposed to realizing that my mistakes resulted from something desperately wrong with who I was on the inside. I saw the manifestation of my sin as fruit on a tree that could be dealt with through a little more self-effort. I was oblivious to the deep roots of my sin — reaching all the way to my childhood — which were the real precipitating problem and made me who I was. I also believe I minimized — albeit not having the framework in my life at the time to understand and comprehend — the harm I had caused those with whom I had been involved. Only later did I come to realize and grieve, through my own healing process, that my position of authority over these young ladies constituted sexual abuse, and contributed to my crimes against them.

I remember people rising to speak one after the other, some in favor and some opposing me. I remember my strange feelings of confusion when my friend spoke the words reflected at the beginning of this chapter. He always believed in me and supported me. I knew he loved me and I could count on him no matter what. He always clothed me with words of encouragement and support, and I guess that's why his words that night felt so strange to me, like trying on a coat you immediately know isn't meant for you because the fit is way too tight. I remember people crying, and I remember being stunned by the most unexpected words that evening. They came from the father of the young lady I had sexual intercourse with. When he arrived at the meeting with his daughter, I remember feeling a sense of terror. I thought he would be raging with anger and wondered if he would physically attack me. I guess my image of him as a father was tinted with the same lens through which I saw my own father — a lens shaded with hues of resentment and anger, bitterness and revenge toward those who have hurt you. As he rose to speak, my eyes fell to the floor in shame, and I braced myself for the onslaught of words that would surely flood over me. But rather than speaking sharp and cutting words filled with contempt, the words he offered were words of grace, seasoned with understanding and forgiveness. He said he believed I was a good young man, full of many gifts and talents, but that I had feet of clay that only proved I was human. He said I made an understandable mistake, and it would be a shame for my gifts to be wasted. He said he had forgiven me for what I had done wrong, and encouraged the entire church to also forgive me and to give me another chance. As he sat down I remember feeling completely numb as words of disbelief spilled from my heart. "I can't believe you. I'm shocked by your words. Of all the people here who should hate me, you should hate me the most, and yet you don't. I can't believe you." It wasn't until years later that I learned the truth concerning the unexpected grace this man demonstrated toward me that evening. Although he knew I had been inappropriately involved with his daughter in some way, he did not know the true extent of what had really happened between us. Years later, when he learned all that had happened, he deeply regretted that he had supported me — and even shook my hand — the night of the church meeting. When he came to understand how much pain I had really caused in his daughter's life, he struggled deeply with a sense of guilt for the rest of his life. When I came to know the understandable truth of this man's feelings toward me, I felt deeply grieved that there was yet another person whose life had been impacted in such a harmful way by my sexual sin.

Then there was the vote, and the anxious minutes that seemed like hours as the count was tallied time and again in the back room. The extended delay was understood when the verdict was finally announced: a dead-even split. For every vote against me there was exactly one vote for me, leaving the church perfectly divided in its conclusion. In a curious twist of fate, this left the final verdict squarely in my lap, as I was the only one who had not yet voted. I knew immediately what I had to do. To close the meeting, I stood and offered my resignation. It was determined that we would immediately disband the church, and each member would be free to begin attending services at the church of his or her choice — and ironically most began attending my pastor's church.

I was 25 years old. I had studied for ministry for 4 years. I believed I was called, and wanted more than anything else to serve God with my life — and I had just lost everything I had worked so hard to gain. My sexual weakness was now public knowledge, and it had brought with it much shame and humiliation for me, and much pain and heartache for others. Although my sin had caused so much trouble, I had no way of knowing I still had a long way to travel on my difficult path.

Chapter 14
Sheri

During the course of the youth group and church I started, a young lady named Jill began attending the meetings. She had recently become a Christian and was excited about spiritual things. On Easter Sunday, 1982, Jill brought her sister Sheri to church. Sheri was not a Christian at the time but wanted to attend church on Easter Sunday. When I met Sheri, little did I know I was encountering one of the greatest gifts God would ever bring into my life, and that she would one day become my wife. In retrospect I see a kind of divine poetry in God allowing us to meet on Easter Sunday — the Christian celebration of God's ability to bring life out of death — and an image of God's redemptive plan for our lives as He brought us together.

As mentioned, our ministry held weekly social events, and although Sheri wasn't interested at the time in attending church services or Bible studies, she did begin hanging out with our group at these various activities. I remember one particular picnic we had after church one Sunday. The whole gang was there, and Sheri showed up with her sister. I remember asking her if she wanted to play catch with me, and as we threw a softball back and forth, something in my heart became completely captured by this young beauty. I remember thinking how beautiful she was in her blue outfit, and I remember being impressed with her ability to throw a softball more like a guy than a girl. In the years ahead I would come to refer to this game of catch as when I began falling in love with Sheri.

In the days that followed the picnic, I found myself frequently thinking about her, and anxiously anticipating her presence at various events. I would ask her sister Jill if Sheri was going to visit, and I encouraged Jill to invite Sheri to the various activities. My infatuation with Sheri continued to grow each time I was around her, and in a short matter of time I asked her if she wanted to have dinner with me. At the time Sheri didn't understand the purpose of my invitation and asked her sister with bewilderment, "Why in the world would your pastor want to have dinner with me?" Jill assured her that I had asked her out only because I was the pastor of the church and it was my job to visit with the new people and make them feel welcome. When the subject came up during our dinner, I told Sheri my interest in her was on a more personal level, and I told her I would really like to spend more time with her. A few days later we played racquetball, and after that we began dating regularly.

Since I was a pastor, and Sheri was not a Christian yet, I was in a kind of precarious position. I knew in my heart that if I were to have any kind of serious relationship with this girl, she would need to become a Christian and become more involved with the church. I had the personal conviction that God would not want me to be unequally yoked with an unbeliever, and I knew I would be seriously judged as a leader if I was perceived by the Christian community as being personally involved with a non-Christian girl. Beyond that, I saw my purpose and calling in life to be involved in ministry, and I knew that any girl I became seriously involved with would also have to love God and want to serve Him. I therefore made Sheri my personal mission field, and began to earnestly pray for her salvation.

As we continued to spend time together, I began sharing more of my faith and the gospel with Sheri. I shared with her that Jesus had died on the cross for her sins, that He rose from the dead 3 days later, and that she could become a child of God and have the free gift of eternal life if she would receive Jesus Christ as her personal Savior. I explained that doing good works had nothing to do with her salvation, and that the only thing she could do to be saved was to accept by faith the free gift of God's love through what Jesus had done for her. The fact that she was beginning to understand the gospel became evident by the questions she began to ask me. Questions like, "You mean to tell me that even my sweet little grandma would go to hell if she didn't have Jesus as her Savior?"

Over a short period of time, as the power of the gospel began to woo her heart, it became my privilege to lead Sheri to the Lord one evening as we sat together on the same lawn chair on her parents' driveway. I gave her the gospel again, and led her to a decision as I asked her if she would like to go ahead and ask Jesus to be her Savior. She said she would, and as I led her in prayer, she silently followed and asked Jesus to come into her heart, to take away her sins, and to be her Savior. In that precious moment, Sheri passed from death unto life, she became a child of God, and she became my sister in Christ. I rejoiced in Sheri's salvation and saw it as a stepping-stone in the possibility of our continued relationship. I had no idea, however, how God would use her life as a sharp scalpel in His hand, like a Master Surgeon, to begin the deep surgery in my heart that was so necessary for the freedom of my own wounded sexuality.

Chapter 15
A Shaky Foundation

 As Sheri and I started our relationship and then entered our marriage, I had no way of understanding we were both deeply wounded and each carried excess baggage from our pasts — baggage like abuse, pain, shame, and self-protection. In hindsight I believe there were several disturbing realities that contributed to the shaky foundation our marriage was founded upon, and that doomed our marriage for certain failure almost from the beginning.

First, a significant part of my own soul was imprisoned in the darkness of sexual bondage, and I made the terrible mistake — among many others — of seeing Sheri as the solution to my dilemma. Although we sincerely loved each other and wanted to spend the rest of our lives together, I believe in retrospect our decision to marry was rushed and no doubt influenced by the collapse of Canaan. I knew I had struggled deeply with my sexual weakness for many years. I knew I had failed over and over again, and now my sexual failure was public knowledge. My weakness had caused me to lose my ministry and hurt many people. Although I do not remember consciously contemplating such a thing, I believe I decided in my own heart that marriage would be the solution to my problem. I must have thought, "After all, since sex has been such a big struggle in my life and caused me so much trouble, if I get married, my sexual problems will be solved because I will be able to have all the sex I want, and it won't even be wrong." I think I may have also unconsciously thought that getting married would be a kind of peace offering to the

Christian community I had so offended, and be a stepping-stone toward the possibility of my restoration to ministry some time in the future. Of course, these foolish musings could not have been any further from the truth, although they were no doubt alive in my own heart as we announced our engagement and were married within six months of Canaan's demise. In reality I placed on Sheri the incredibly unfair expectation to be the solution to the problem of my own sick soul — something she couldn't have been even if she wanted to. I would learn in time, through the profoundly difficult healing process God would require of me, that *He* alone could redeem my sexuality from the dark prison that held it captive — that *He* alone was the answer to my dilemma. He — and not the "torch" of marriage I chose to light in an attempt to make my own way through the darkness that surrounded me — would be my salvation.

> Let him who walks in the dark, who has no light, trust in the name of the LORD and rely on his God. But now, all you who light fires and provide for yourselves with flaming torches, go, walk in the light of your fires and of the torches you have set ablaze. This is what you shall receive from my hand: You will lie down in torment. Isaiah 50:10–11

Another factor that contributed to the doubtful foundation of our marriage was the conspicuous absence of any voice of reason or admonition that might have warned us to slow down and proceed with caution given the less-than-desirable circumstances that surrounded the commencement of our relationship. In hindsight, as Sheri and I have talked about this, we cannot believe that someone from the company of people that surrounded us did not take out a red flag, wave it in our faces, and throw an absolute fit because of how quickly we made such life-changing decisions. In fairness, my sister-in-law says she and my brother tried to warn me to slow down and re-evaluate the direction I was moving, but for the life of me I do not remember any such discussion. I don't know if that's because they were so gentle in their approach, or if it's because my head was so hard I couldn't even hear what they were trying to say. Regardless, Sheri and I did not recognize any such voice of reason around us and we continued moving forward.

As a final ingredient to the uncertain foundation of our marriage, Sheri and I were apparently completely oblivious to one another's faults. They say that love is blind, and if that's true, we must have really been in love, because we were really blind! Of course, since Sheri was so young and just a brand-

A Shaky Foundation   79

new Christian, she really didn't have any frame of reference that might have warned her against moving forward in her relationship with me. If she would have had such a perspective, she could have easily thought to herself, "I better slow down and attempt to understand more of what causes this man Tony to tick. I see some warning signs here that give me reason to be suspicious. He's a Christian and a pastor of this little church, and yet when it comes to our physical relationship he treats me virtually the same as all the other guys I've dated. Not only that, but now I've discovered along with everybody else that he's recently been involved physically with these other young ladies, and he's losing his church over it. This is really a very serious matter, and I wonder if he's in fact the kind of man I want to commit the rest of my life to. Hmmmm."

In the absence of such an appropriate voice of reason, Sheri didn't recognize the evidence that should have alerted her, and she continued to naively progress in her relationship with me. In much the same way, although I was 4 years older than Sheri and had been a Christian for at least 8 years, and although I knew much of Sheri's difficult background and history, I simply didn't understand how such issues from the past could so deeply affect a person's future and marriage. It's as though Sheri and I were at an amusement park together and we decided to get in line to experience the new monster ride, MARRIAGE! As we passed through the turnstile by saying "I do" to one another, then naively boarded side by side, we had no way of knowing how wild the ride was going to be.

Chapter 16
Unrealistic Expectations

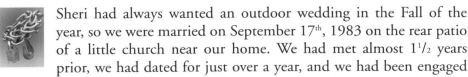
Sheri had always wanted an outdoor wedding in the Fall of the year, so we were married on September 17th, 1983 on the rear patio of a little church near our home. We had met almost 1 1/2 years prior, we had dated for just over a year, and we had been engaged for 6 months. As our wedding day approached, I was excited at the prospect of spending the rest of my life with the girl I loved, and filled with the anticipation of making love as much and as often as we wanted. After struggling so deeply with my sexuality for so long, the expectation of being able to have all the sex I wanted, without it being wrong or without suffering any consequences, seemed too good to be true. I had an idyllic image in my mind of the two of us as hungry young lovers, who would feed one another over and over again from a kind of smorgasbord of love that would include such delicacies as tenderness, romance, and passion. I imagined us in the lushness of our own little Eden, enraptured with one another's presence, irresistibly attracted to one another, each adoring the other as the darling of our eyes. My expectations of our marriage and intimate relationship although lofty indeed, were completely misguided. So imagine my confusion and disorientation when Sheri was both emotionally and physically shut down, not only on our wedding night, but also for the months and years that would follow. It would be many years later, after unimaginable heartache and pain, that I would begin to understand how the combination of Sheri's

past and the man I was as her husband, worked together as allies against her in the very real war that was raging in her soul.

In fact, in much the same way the development of my own sexuality was surrounded by less-than-ideal circumstances and influences, Sheri's own development in this area of her life was also deeply troubled. As a cumulative result of various influences on her young life, it's as though some empty and lonely place deep in Sheri's heart was desperately screaming by the time she was an adolescent, "Somebody please notice me! Somebody please pay attention to me! Somebody please delight in me! Somebody please love me!" As a consequence, Sheri was left in the dangerous position as a young lady to begin looking in all the wrong places for the love, affection, and attention she so deeply craved. As a result of her vulnerability, Sheri naively and unknowingly turned to numerous broken cisterns in her attempt to quench the kind of thirsty longing that lived in her soul. This misguided search in turn led to a series of terrible events in Sheri's life, including being raped — which was her first sexual experience — when she was 14 years old and having an abortion at the age of 18. In her search to fill the empty and lonely place in her heart, she naturally turned to boys, and as she did, she quickly learned that the boys she came into contact with were typically after the same thing from her. At such a young age, and without the benefit of a healthier frame of reference, it was easy for Sheri to mistakenly confuse the physical attention of boys for the true love and intimacy she genuinely desired. Therefore, at times, although she felt an underlying sense of shame somewhere deep in her conscience, she nevertheless allowed herself to be taken advantage of in ways she would later come to regret deeply.

Given this brief background of Sheri's history, and knowing what you already know regarding my history, you might begin to see how the two of us were headed for trouble from the very beginning. You'd think — or hope at least — that once Sheri met me everything would have been different for her. Since I was a Christian, and the pastor of a church, you'd think I would have conducted myself appropriately in our relationship. You'd think that during the course of our dating relationship I would have been radically different from the other guys she had dated, by respecting her and by keeping our physical relationship on a level that would honor both her and the Lord. But unfortunately, and much to my own shame, I failed Sheri very deeply while we were dating by conducting myself in much the same way as many of her previous boyfriends. Because of the weakness in the sexual area of my own life, I began to pursue Sheri physically, and after dating for a short matter of time we became sexually involved. Sheri was not even a Christian yet, and through the progress of our relationship, which included the downfall of my ministry and our speedy engagement, one event happened that stands out in my mind.

I had led Sheri to the Lord several months prior, and Canaan had come to an end. We were engaged at the time, and we were sexually active. I think I justified my behavior through reasoning that we were engaged, we were going to be married in a short matter of time, and then sex would be legal for us anyway. I'd say to myself, "After all, marriage isn't really a piece of paper that says you're married. It's a commitment between the hearts of two people. Since we're already committed to one another, it's really all right if we make love because we're already married in the eyes of God anyway." In spite of such convenient reasoning and my best attempts to persuade Sheri accordingly, I began to nevertheless detect in her a growing conscience against our sexual activity. It's as though Sheri innately knew from her unfortunate past that she should not be having sex or allowing men to take advantage of her, and now that she had become a Christian, her newly awakened conscience — and the Holy Spirit — were both speaking to her louder than ever before. Although she had been gently resisting my advances, I initiated toward her on one particular instance, and she responded by telling me she did not want to have sex with me again until we were married because she felt like it was wrong. Unfortunately, instead of respecting and agreeing with her proper desire, I proceeded to differ with her and negotiate for what I wanted. I told Sheri that if we could have sex just this once more before we got married, that we would not have sex again until our wedding night. In the end, Sheri reluctantly surrendered to my selfish persistence, and we had sex for the last time before we were married.

As we continued to abstain from further sexual activity for the couple months before our wedding, I eagerly anticipated our wedding night with visions of grandeur similar to those reflected at the beginning of this chapter. In reality, I didn't understand how deeply my self-serving actions had harmed Sheri's delicate conscience, and contributed to the sense of shame she already felt regarding her difficult past. In the years ahead I would eventually come to deeply regret the way I conducted myself toward my young bride-to-be. I would long for the chance to travel back in time and have the opportunity to relive our dating days and engagement. I would yearn for the possibility to do so many things differently: to honor Sheri by my willingness to wait until marriage to consummate our love; to respect Sheri by controlling my natural desires; and to put her welfare and dignity before my own selfish interests. But despite my desire to rewind time and do things differently, I would be given no such opportunity. In reality, I could not go back in time to change the many mistakes I made along the way, and I could not change the person I was so many years ago. Instead, I would be required to face the future, and a God who was determined to change me from the inside out.

Chapter 17
A Head-on Collision

Our much-awaited wedding day finally arrived, and although I had so anticipated our first night together, it turned out to be completely different from what I expected. When Sheri seemed almost reluctant to make love with me, I figured she was just tired from the excitement of such an important and busy day. It's as if her body was there physically, but the real Sheri was somehow absent. I thought things would be better in the days ahead, but in reality things went from bad to worse. Sheri simply shut down emotionally and physically, and seemed incapable of responding to me. In a very short matter of time our physical relationship was virtually non-existent, and it wasn't unusual for prolonged periods of time to pass between our sexual encounters. At one point in our marriage a period of nine months elapsed between our physical intimacies, and although that was the longest such period of time, it wasn't unusual for many months to separate such encounters. Shortly after our wedding, our marriage wasn't a picture of two people blending into one. Instead, it was more like a head-on crash of two people's diametrically opposed sexual points of reference.

On one hand, Sheri had been treated as more of an object than a person by most of the males she had been in relationships with. It's as if her history had created within her a growing sense of resentment toward being treated in such a way, and she therefore found it increasingly difficult to respond or give herself to a man she sensed was more interested in her body than respecting her as a person. On the other hand, my history shaped within me an exaggerated level of sexual energy and expectation, and caused me to see my wife more as a sexual object to be used than as a person to be respected. Of course, these divergent points of view regarding what each of us wanted, expected, and thought we needed from the other aligned us utterly opposite of one another, and set us up to be bitterly disappointed in what the other person had to offer. In reality we were both completely incapable at the time of providing for one another that which we each so desperately wanted and needed.

Although I did love Sheri and respected her to the best of my ability at the time, and although I did choose to give my life to her through marriage, it was also painfully true that my attitudes, feelings, and expectations regarding sex were more often than not misguided and inappropriate. There was a definite excess of sexual energy alive in my soul — an ugliness with its roots all the way back to my childhood — and a wrongness that served to push Sheri away from me rather than attract her toward me. Although Sheri wasn't completely innocent and there were genuine issues she would have to face in the days ahead regarding how she had also deeply failed me, the fact remained that a woman would find it difficult to respond to the kind of man I was. Like a sleeping bear might slowly stir after a long and cold winter's hibernation, it's as if Sheri's sense of dignity and self-respect was being roused after being dormant for so many years, and she understandably found it difficult to respond to the kind of man I was as her husband.

These were only the beginning days of what would prove to be an incredibly dark and difficult process God was going to take our marriage through, and it would be years before we would begin to understand and believe how, in the most peculiar and unbelievable way, God created us perfectly for one another! In time we would come to see how the Valley of the Shadow of Death that God would require our marriage to go through, and the profoundly difficult and painful process of being so utterly hurt by and disappointed in one another, would become the very tools God would use to begin to change each of us from the inside out, and to make us into a man and woman perfectly suited for one another.

Unbeknownst to me, God, as the Master Surgeon, had taken a sharp scalpel named Sheri into His hand to be the very tool He would use to cut deeply into my soul to begin delivering me from the cancer of my sexual bondage and the chains that had held me captive for so long. Likewise, God would use the sharp scalpel of my life to assault the ugliness of sin that lived within my wife. In an unfolding drama, despite our conflicting viewpoints regarding our sexual relationship and the resulting pain and heartache, we would come to ultimately see the fingerprints of God on our lives through the arduous upcoming days.

CHAPTER 18

EMOTIONAL
REVOLT

As weeks became months, and months became years, our marriage continued down a dark and desperate path and relentlessly assaulted my out-of-proportion sexuality. As Sheri remained imprisoned by the emotional and spiritual bondages that held her captive, including her unfortunate past and the reality of living with the kind of man I was as her husband, she remained hopelessly paralyzed in her ability to respond to me. As a result of the almost torturous course on which our marriage was progressing, or better said floundering, an inevitable and vast sense of distance came to define our relationship, and a cycle began in my life that would repeat itself over and over for years to come. I later came to refer to this cycle as "emotional revolt." This cycle consisted of a cast of horrible members, including denial, depression, frustration, anger, acting out, guilt, shame, and renewed determination. Although they appeared in varying sequence, each member of the troupe took its place at various times on the center stage of my life.

The progression of this cycle generally began with my head and my heart engaged in a significant level of denial. I had absolutely no idea what to do about our failing marriage, and felt completely and hopelessly incapable of changing the situation. Armed with a sense of such powerlessness and incompetence, I resorted to doing the next best thing, and the only other thing I felt I could do — nothing! Incapable of seeing any solutions to our painful and unpromising dilemma, and being met with utter failure any time I did

89

attempt to improve our relationship, I learned that the best way to deal with the circumstances of our marriage was not to deal with them at all. I therefore typically did my best to ignore the difficult realities of our marriage, pretending like things were not as bad as they really were, and distracting myself with other activities and interests that offered me a greater sense of control and satisfaction than my marriage. At, or very near the top of my "it's easier to focus and spend energy on this than it is to face my horrible marriage and home life" list, became my job. Since I had always been an effective communicator and enjoyed meeting new people, a sales career suited me perfectly, and within the first year of our marriage I found a sales position with a local remodeling company. From the very beginning of my career in sales I did exceptionally well, made more money than I had ever made in my life, and enjoyed the accompanying sense of respect, accomplishment, and self-gratification that came with such success. Given such a rewarding environment at work compared to the lack of control and disappointment I felt in the context of my marriage, it became natural for me to direct more and more of my energies toward my career, and within a few short years of our marriage I started my own remodeling company. I went on to own that company for almost 10 years, and because of the energy I invested in it — in large part as a way of distracting myself from the difficult circumstances confronting me at home — it eventually grew, with the help of the good people I had hired as co-laborers, into one of the largest remodeling companies in the St. Louis area and the entire Midwest.

Although I did my best to ignore the circumstances of my marriage, and distracted myself with work and the pursuit of "success," like living under a dark and ominous cloud that never went away, there was almost always a slumbering sense of depression and despair waiting to rouse itself and swallow me whole. I could normally keep myself preoccupied with this distracted manner of denial for anywhere from weeks to several months, all the while keeping the depression and ensuing cycle of "emotional revolt" at arm's length. However, despite my best efforts to manage my life and make it work in the face of such difficulties, in due course I came face-to-face with the terrible reality of our lives and inevitably collapsed into a serious depression. Such episodes could be triggered by any number of precipitating events, including such things as having a difficult confrontation with Sheri, seeing another seemingly happy couple, struggling with feelings of loneliness and sexual frustration, or even watching a movie with the common theme of "guy gets girl and lives happily ever after." Regardless of the cause, such periods of depression inevitably overcame me as the convenience and protection of my distracted denial abandoned me.

The ensuing period of depression would last anywhere from days to weeks, or even months, and was accompanied at times by radical thoughts and feelings, such as an overwhelming sense of hopelessness and despair, and destructive thoughts that included fantasies of divorce, suicide, and even murder. In retrospect, I recognize that many of the harmful and venomous thoughts and impulses that assaulted me during these periods of dark despair and anguish had their heinous origins from the sinister pits of hell itself, as the enemy of my soul sought to completely destroy my marriage, my family, and my life. "Be self-controlled and alert. Your enemy the devil prowls around like a roaring lion looking for someone to devour" (I Peter 5:8).

Make no mistake, and do not be lullabied into believing that there is not a very real enemy who is seeking to utterly and completely destroy your family and your very life, in the same way he was trying to destroy mine. It was in these darkest of days that the devil attempted to bring his vile handiwork in our lives to completion — handiwork he had begun years earlier through tools like pornography, rape, abuse, abortion, and promiscuity. The cumulative effect of these despicable influences in our lives served to estrange Sheri and I from one another, and like a gigantic wedge driven between us, made it impossible for us to relate to one another intimately. The resulting feelings of depression, hopelessness, and despair made life itself, at times, seem completely unbearable or desirable. Apart from God's grace protecting us, and maybe a little stubborn tenacity on our parts reflected by our refusal to give up on a marriage that many people would have surrendered long ago, I shudder to think how close we were at times to losing the war that was waging in our lives.

In time, the monster of depression that gripped me so tightly would yield to emerging feelings of frustration and outright anger or rage. It was at these times I was the most dangerous, and my extreme feelings led to inappropriate behaviors, including punishing Sheri with silence for periods of up to weeks at a time, avoiding home by going out with friends numerous nights in a row, threatening Sheri with divorce and promising her that I was going to commit adultery, and even having a couple physical outbursts that included smashing chairs and other household items into the walls of our home. Although these manifestations of my anger and internal struggle were bad enough, my emotional revolt reached its pinnacle when my anger turned toward God Himself, and I would raise my clenched fist to shake it defiantly in His face. I would question God, yell at God, and curse God. I couldn't understand who He was or where He was. I couldn't understand why He seemed so far away and so completely unconcerned about my life or my pain. I couldn't understand why He wouldn't do something to help our desperate situation when I had asked Him and begged Him to help us so many times. I knew in my head the theology I had learned in Bible college — that God is a God of love, that He wants to have a personal relationship with His children, that He knew the very number of hairs on my head, and that all things work together to good for those who love God and are called according to His purpose (Romans 8:28).

But the God I knew about in my head, and the God I knew in my heart and my real life experience seemed diametrically different from one another. One was supposed to love me and care for me; the other seemed to care less. One was supposed to be my strength and my helper; the other seemed powerless. One was supposed to see and hear; the other seemed blind and deaf. And one was supposed to desire my love and devotion, but the other seemed to be a distant and aloof lover.

As I struggled with my confusion, I would live many years and cry many tears before I would begin to slowly gain the proper perspective that the God of love, in an unexpected and mysterious way, is also the God of destruction. I learned that the true God of love, as the Master Surgeon, would be constrained to set aside my comfort and my happiness for the greater purpose of cutting me deeply in the effort to deliver me from a hideous cancer infecting my soul and depriving me of true life.

It was during these recalcitrant days in the depths of emotional revolt that my behavior became the most treacherous. I was angry with Sheri, I was angry with God, and I came to the terrible place — although I knew right from wrong — of simply not caring. It was with this insolent attitude of defiance and rebellion that I determined to extract revenge upon those whom I was so bitterly disappointed with, and punish them by acting out accordingly. These episodes included surrendering completely to thoughts of lust and masturbation, visiting strip clubs several times, flirting with other women, and committing adultery. Feelings of guilt, conviction, and shame normally quickly followed the collapse of my moral infrastructure, and I would purpose to straighten myself up as I renewed my determination to do the right thing. I would then refocus my energy on work, as the familiar friend of my distracted denial took its cue for center stage, thus completing my predictable cycle of emotional revolt.

Chapter 19
Unfaithfulness & Betrayal

 While in the deep abyss of emotional revolt, fueled by the dark energy provided by such base motivations as sexual frustration, anger, revenge, and rebellion, I seemed powerless to resist temptation and incapable of doing the right thing. I promised Sheri many times in anger, and no doubt as a way of threatening her, that I was going to have an affair. I'd tell her I could not live without sex, that it was only a matter of time, and that the question was *when* I would fail rather than *if* I would fail. I complained that what Sheri was doing to me was unfair, that she was my wife, and it was her duty to have sex with me; and I frequently bludgeoned her with verses from the Bible that conveyed her sexual responsibility to me. Of course, all these attempts to control Sheri and manipulate her were completely ineffective, and in fact only served to widen the deep chasm that separated our hearts and our bodies from one another. I therefore busied myself with my familiar friend of distracted denial until the darkness of emotional revolt belched its vileness from the depths of my soul. It was at these times I entered the perilous phase of simply not caring what was right or wrong, and even looked for the opportunity to do the improper thing. When I consider, in retrospect, my motives and my actions at such times, it's as though I thought — regardless of how crazy it sounds — that the retaliation of my acting out would somehow make those with whom I was so bitterly disappointed — namely Sheri and God — "pay" and somehow thus relieve the anguish of my own suffering soul. What I failed to recognize at the time is how completely deceived I really was, and how the enemy of my soul was luring me deeper into his trap, like a wild wolf enticed by the smell of fresh blood[1], as he nurtured his plan to completely destroy my life. It was at such periods I stooped to the treachery of betrayal and the ugliness of adultery.

Although I struggled deeply with lust toward other women, and committed adultery in my heart thousands of times (Matthew 5:27–28), the first time I committed adultery outwardly was at the end of our second year of marriage. I met a woman through a business situation, and she conveyed to me in no uncertain terms her availability. I was well acquainted with the "vibe" by this time, and this woman was sending signals loud and clear.

> She took hold of him and kissed him and with a brazen face she said: "I have fellowship offerings at home; today I fulfilled my vows. So I came out to meet you; I looked for you and have found you! I have covered my bed with colored linens from Egypt. I have perfumed my bed with myrrh, aloes and cinnamon. Come, let's drink deep of love till morning; let's enjoy ourselves with love!" Proverbs 7:13–18

Unfortunately, I was in the sad place of being completely vulnerable to such temptation, and willfully reached for the forbidden fruit that had been placed before me. "All at once he followed her like an ox going to the slaughter, like a deer stepping into a noose till an arrow pierces his liver, like a bird darting into a snare, little knowing it would cost him his life" (Proverbs 7:22–23).

Although I was in the terrible mindset of wanting a full-blown affair with this woman, in the end we only had one liaison. It was only later I learned she was in fact having an affair with another married man who had been promising her he was going to leave his wife and marry her. It was on the heels of a bitter fight with him that she made herself available to me. In an ironic twist of fate, instead of punishing others through my misdeed, I was instead used as a pawn by a seductive woman intent on extracting revenge on the duplicitous man in her life.

Although this adulterous rendezvous was bad enough, it was at least very brief compared to my two other entanglements. The first was a kind of emotional affair that simmered in my heart for many years toward none other than Sheri's older sister. For a number of reasons that seem better left unmentioned, I found myself infatuated with my sister-in-law, and struggled deeply in my heart with inappropriate thoughts and desires toward her. Although I believe the energy and attraction between us was mutual, I must give her credit for not allowing anything of extreme significance to happen between the two of us outwardly. Although there were inappropriate flirtations, and we did actually kiss once, it was because of her refusal to move forward that nothing of more consequence happened between us.

The other intrigue I participated in also started with a kind of powerful attraction, but quickly exploded into much more. The very sad truth that added insult to injury for everyone involved is that this unfortunate and terrible situation involved a couple of our very close friends. Although I knew what I was allowing to happen was terribly wrong, at times I seemed completely powerless to resist the compelling temptation that swept over me, and I surrendered accordingly. This unfortunate situation continued for 5 years, as I struggled deeply with my vicious cycles of moral failure — God understands, God will forgive me, and I'll never do it again; the Tasmanian Devil; and emotional revolt. Whenever something happened between us, I almost immediately felt overwhelmed with guilt and shame, and I hated myself for allowing such a thing to happen. On such occasions I scolded myself over and over with such reprimands as, "Tony, you stupid idiot! What is wrong with you? How could you allow yourself to do such a thing? What kind of person are you? How could you do such a thing to one of your closest friends? What if everybody finds out? What will you do? You've already made a public spectacle of yourself by losing Canaan. Can you imagine what people will think if they find out about this? What if Sheri finds out? What if your kids find out? What if your friend finds out? What if the church finds out? You better straighten yourself up and never, ever let this happen again!" I would then plead to God, "Please, God! Help me! Please forgive me and help me to never do this again!"

Next, I would attempt to push the ever-present temptation away from me, force the Tasmanian Devil back into his fragile cage, and purpose to never let such a thing happen again. I would then exert my best effort to manage my life and control my exaggerated sexuality, which was obviously more powerful than even my best effort. I would typically be successful for a period ranging anywhere from weeks to several months, but inevitably my life would sequence back to the place of coming face-to-face with the horrible reality of my difficult marriage, and I would spiral back into the depths of emotional revolt. Empowered at such times by dark forces of depression, anger, and revenge, I would typically reach once again for the forbidden fruit I mistakenly thought would somehow give respite to my troubled soul. Once I had so failed, guilt and shame would cascade over me like a waterfall, and the cycle would begin again — an adulterous cycle that repeated itself approximately ten times during this 5-year period.

These tragic events represent the deepest failures of my life, and embody the culmination of the devil's effort to destroy my marriage and my life through my broken and misguided sexuality. They are among the most shameful and reprehensible things I have ever done, and represent that which I most wish I could change regarding my past mistakes. Even now, as I write these words, I cannot believe I would allow myself to sink so low as to be able or willing to so deeply hurt and offend those closest to me, including my wife, members of my family, my friends, and God Himself. If there is anything of redemptive value that could emerge from such tragedy, it is simply God's wondrous ability to rescue those whom have hit rock bottom.

---

1 I once heard a sermon illustration that graphically and powerfully illustrates how completely deceived we are when we willfully choose to disobey God and chase after the sin we mistakenly believe will satisfy the longing of our hungry hearts. The preacher told of an ingenious ploy the Eskimos of old used to fool the wits of the cagey wolf, and lure him to his own demise. Knowing their adversary's natural affinity and craving for the taste of blood, the Eskimos cunningly used the wolf's innate desire and keen sense of smell against him. In the sub-zero temperatures in which they lived, they would take a razor-sharp, two-edged blade and dip it repeatedly in a reservoir of blood. The frigid temperature would instantly freeze the consecutive layers of blood over the lethal instrument, and with repetitive dipping, the crafty hunter soon created a kind of blood popsicle. He would then take his deadly bait into the wild, affix it to a tree or stump, and leave it there to accomplish its gruesome handiwork. In a matter of time, the unsuspecting wolf would wander by and, enticed by the irresistible aroma of the tempting lure, approach to investigate. Unable to resist the delicious and convenient offering, the wolf would smell and then begin to slowly lick his tasty prize. As his hot breath and warm mouth came in contact with the bloodsicle, it would gradually melt in his mouth, providing the wolf with the increasing satisfaction of his favorite taste. In a short matter of time, with the smell in his nostrils and the taste of fresh blood in his mouth, the wolf would begin to lick the blood pop with frenzied delight, and would soon reach the razor-sharp blade at the heart of his fatal banquet. By this time, intoxicated with the flavor of warm blood flowing over his tongue and down his throat, the wolf would proceed to slash his own tongue and face to shreds as he passionately labored to consume every tasty drop of blood — little realizing the blood he was now consuming had become his very own! When the Eskimo would return to check his deadly trap, he invariably found his foolish quarry lying just a few short yards from the site of his last supper, dead from a multitude of self-inflicted wounds! It seems that in the end, the very thing the wolf thought would satisfy him, and the very thing he pursued with such passion, was the very thing that required him to pay with his life. "There is a way that seems right to a man, but in the end it leads to death" (Proverbs 14:12).

Section 2

The Ascending Journey & Freedom

Chapter 20

Divine
Desperation

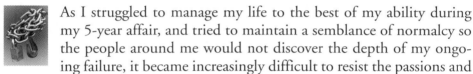As I struggled to manage my life to the best of my ability during my 5-year affair, and tried to maintain a semblance of normalcy so the people around me would not discover the depth of my ongoing failure, it became increasingly difficult to resist the passions and forces that attempted to command my obedience and pull me into the swirling vortex of their power. With each subsequent round of emotional revolt and corresponding failure — like Superman after he had been exposed to kryptonite — I felt weakened in my ability or power to fight back. I felt myself sinking lower and lower into the powerful undertow that held me captive and was trying to suck me under, and I had a growing feeling of desperation as I sensed my inability to hold my head above water.

Although the details of my scandalous 5-year affair were dark enough, I held as one redeeming point of light the fact that I had not yet had sexual intercourse with the woman I was involved with. As crazy as it sounds, I was determined not to cross that particular line, and when I felt overwhelmed with guilt because of my involvement with her, I solaced myself by remembering that at least I hadn't allowed myself to consummate our relationship. I used this vain reasoning in an attempt to minimize my sense of guilt, as I justified that although what we were doing was bad enough, it could always be worse. It's as if I used what we had not done to make myself feel less guilty about the things we had done. The dilemma of my terrible situation was therefore further complicated when my intuition began warning me — like a red flashing light at a dangerous intersection — that it would only be a short matter of time before we would cross that final line. I knew the affair was progressing down a one-way street, and since we were moving dangerously closer to its natural end with each encounter, I sensed it would be a short while before we arrived at the final destination of intercourse. The thought of this possibility struck terror in my heart because I knew myself, and sensed that if such a thing were allowed to occur, I would then completely surrender to a full-blown affair with her that would inevitably be discovered. I knew I could not allow such a thing to happen, and yet I was tormented because I recognized I was incapable of keeping this obvious conclusion from occurring. It was in the face of this hopeless impasse that I truly began to realize for the first time, deep within my soul, how completely powerless I was over my own sexuality.

Up until that moment, and in spite of my many failures over the years, I had somehow managed to deceive myself into believing that my problem wasn't as bad as it really was. I saw myself as a basically good person who had this moral blemish that surfaced occasionally and caused a deep struggle in my life. Although I knew my actions were wrong, I minimized the severity of my problem, and justified myself by rationalizing that all men, including my father and my pastor, struggle with such things. Even King David himself had the same weakness. I often thought that God understood my weakness and — like a traffic cop who pulls someone over for speeding and then releases him with just a warning — was willing to look the other way despite my moral failings. After all, I reasoned, I did try to do the right thing most of the time, I was sincerely trying to serve God to the best of my ability, and it was only in moments of weakness that I failed and made mistakes. Little did I realize how deeply deceived I had been for so many years as I minimized the failures of my life by framing them from an unhealthy point of reference that didn't make me look so bad. As the Bible says in Jeremiah 17:9, "The heart is deceitful above all things and beyond cure. Who can understand it?"

In spite of my all-too-convenient denial, I was forced to come face-to-face with the reality of my utter desperation. My circumstances became a kind of mirror, and when I was forced to look at them honestly, I saw the reflection of a man completely out of control. It was at this point the picture of the Tasmanian Devil first occurred to me, and I realized that no matter how hard I tried, I would NEVER be able to win my battle against him. Like a hard slap in the face, my realization became crystal clear that although I might be able to resist him for limited periods of time, he was more powerful than me, and he could essentially require my allegiance to him at any time. I couldn't lie to myself anymore. I couldn't pretend that my problem wasn't really that bad. I couldn't pretend any longer that I had control of my sexuality, when in reality it had control of me. The circumstances of my terrible situation forced me to admit that I was completely powerless and my life was out of my control. I began to realize that my good intentions, my desire to do the right thing, and my very best efforts at self-control were all meaningless. I knew that no matter how hard I tried, it would only be a matter of time before I would fail again. I was seeing that I was not bigger than life, but that life was bigger than me. My sexuality was holding me in bondage, and because of my slavery I was in the process of destroying everything in my life that meant the very most to me, including my marriage, my family, my friendships, and my Christianity.

As my soul comprehended these realities one after the other, like giant and powerful waves pushed by the violence of a coming hurricane, I felt an overwhelming sense of panic; a panic I would later come to refer to as "divine desperation." Although this place of fearful honesty was a terrible and dark threshold to cross, I would eventually come to see it as the first strategic step of my healing process[1]. "On hearing this, Jesus said, 'It is not the healthy who need a doctor, but the sick. But go and learn what this means: 'I desire mercy, not sacrifice.' For I have not come to call the righteous, but sinners'" (Matthew 9:12).

Before God could begin to heal my life and redeem the brokenness of my sexuality, I had to come to the humble place of truly admitting how desperately needy and sick I really was. I needed to repent of the hypocrisy of pretending to be a man who was in control of his life and his sexuality. I needed to repent of the deceptive charade and duplicity of presenting myself as one man, when in reality I was a very different man. According to God's Word, I needed to come to the place where I would first admit the truth to myself: "If we claim to be without sin, we deceive ourselves and the truth is not in us" (I John 1:8), and "Surely you desire truth in the inner parts; you teach me the wisdom in inmost place" (Psalm 51:6). Only after I admitted the truth to myself could I then agree with God regarding my sin: "If we confess our sins, he is faithful and just and will forgive us our sins and purify us from all unrighteousness" (I John 1:9). Only then, finally, could I admit the truth to others: "If we claim to have fellowship with him yet walk in the darkness, we lie and do not live by the truth. But if we walk in the light, as he is in the light, we have fellowship with one another, and the blood of Jesus, his Son, purifies us from all sin" (I John 1:6–7).

Although the searing light of truth is painful and blinding to those whose eyes have adjusted long ago to groping in darkness, I knew from scripture that God seems to work His best when people have finally reached the end of themselves, arriving at a place of "divine desperation." Among many other Biblical examples, there was the prodigal son, whose hungry belly provided the impetus for him to begin his journey back to his father (Luke 15:1–20); the woman with the issue of blood, whose condition only worsened after she spent all she had on many doctors and was thus compelled to seek the hem of Jesus' garment (Mark 5:24–34); and the lonely blind man, whose despair constrained him to cry out with reckless abandon for Jesus when everyone around him told him to be quiet (Luke 18:35–43).

In much the same way, coming face-to-face with the overwhelming reality of my sexual bondage — and my complete powerlessness and inability to do anything about it — caused something deep in my heart to break and I became more aware of my desperate need for God than ever before. I realized for the first time that I needed God to save me, not just from my sin — the things I had done wrong — but I needed God to save me from myself — the very essence of who I was as a person[2]. I was more desperate than I had ever been. I knew the stakes at this crossroads of my life were incredibly high, and although I was more scared than I had ever been, I could sense God was calling me to take His hand and step into the light of truth. I knew beyond a shadow of a doubt that if I continued to fight my battle alone, it would only be a matter of time before I would fail and all would be lost. I somehow knew the only way I could stop that from happening is if I did something I never imagined I would be able to do — I had to tell on myself!

---

1 In his devotional book, *My Utmost For His Highest,* Oswald Chambers writes in the entry for November 28th:

> We have to realize that we cannot earn or win anything from God through our own efforts. We must either receive it as a gift or do without it. The greatest spiritual blessing we receive is when we come to the knowledge that we are destitute. Until we get there, our Lord is powerless. He can do nothing for us as long as we think we are sufficient in and of ourselves. We must enter into His kingdom through the door of destitution. As long as we are "rich," particularly in the area of pride or independence, God can do nothing for us. It is only when we get hungry spiritually that we receive the Holy Spirit.

2 In Bible college I learned that there are three phases of my salvation. First is justification, which means I am saved instantly and completely from God's wrath and the penalty of my sins (Romans 5:1). Second is sanctification, which means I am in the process of being saved from the power of sin in my daily life (Phil. 1:6). Third is glorification, which means one day — when I arrive in heaven — I will be saved from the very presence of sin (Revelation 21:27). When we receive Jesus Christ as our personal savior we become a child of God, and although our salvation is instantly complete in Christ, the fullness of that salvation is being worked out progressively in our lives (sanctification) as we walk with Christ each day and He works in us to make us more and more like Jesus.

CHAPTER 21

INNER VOICES & THE HEAVY HAND of God

 I was deeply ambivalent as I contemplated the possibility of revealing my battle to the world. I knew there was only one way to break the power of my sexual bondage, thus changing the quick and dark progress of my affair: expose my affair to the light of truth. This was the only way I could, in a sense, kick my enemy in the face and loosen his tight grip on me. I knew that if the secrecy of the affair was uncovered, it would instantly bring any further contact between the two of us to a grinding halt, thus accomplishing through exposure what I could never accomplish through clandestine self-effort. At the same time, though, I was paralyzed with fear as I considered the possible consequences of such a revelation. I had always been careful to conceal the depth of my real struggle and, like Adam and Eve in the Garden of Eden (Genesis 3:8), I attempted to hide the naked shame of my failure with familiar bushes like minimization, rationalization, and denial.

In one sense it felt ludicrous to entertain for even 1 minute the possibility of bringing to light that which I had always wanted to remain hidden, and part of me protested vehemently as something in my soul shrieked at the thought of being found out. "Tony, are you absolutely crazy? There is no way you can tell anybody about this! Do you realize what it could mean if this is

106 Stories: The Redemption of One Man's Wounded Sexuality

found out? What if Sheri finds out? She might leave you or divorce you! You'll lose your family! And what about the kids? What will your kids think and how will their lives be affected if you get divorced? What about your money? If she divorces you, you'll lose at least half of everything you have! Can you imagine what will happen if your friend finds out about this? How will it make him feel and what will he do? What about their kids? And what about the church? What will you do if everyone in the church finds out what you are really like? They already know about your past, and losing Canaan! And they know you have had terrible problems in your marriage! If people find out about this they will see you as a total failure, and they will blame all your marital problems on you! What about the rest of your family? What about your mom and your dad and all your siblings? They will all be so ashamed of you and so embarrassed by you! Your life will be ruined forever if people find out who you really are! You better keep your big mouth shut!"

As these passionate voices of self-preservation echoed through my soul, I heard another dissenting voice that quietly but persistently encouraged me in the opposite direction. "Tony, you know you have to do this! You have a serious problem and you know you are incapable of dealing with it! It's a problem that's bigger than you, and you have struggled with it for your entire life! If you try to continue battling it on your own, you know what's going to happen! You're going to lose, because you always lose! You might be able to fend it off for awhile, but in a matter of time you will surrender to its power and you will fail once again! You've already blown it and made a huge mess of things, and if you don't get some help the situation is going to go from bad to worse! You better confess the truth to someone and break the power this thing has over you! It's going to be incredibly difficult, but at least you know it's the right thing to do, and God will help you through it! There's no other way out of this mess! You have to confess and seek the help you need!"

While these divergent voices vigorously campaigned against one another, and sought to commandeer my life's direction, I could discern the heavy hand of God on my life. I sensed that my life was at a significant crossroads, and the path I decided upon would have profound implications for the remainder of my days. As each day passed, and I continued to labor under my difficult burden and my looming decision, I had a growing sense of God's presence around me, and I felt that God Himself was bringing pressure to bear upon my soul. At times I felt a tangible heaviness upon me, and as I struggled to make it through each day, there were times I physically had

INNER VOICES & THE HEAVY HAND of God   107

difficulty breathing. I felt an invisible weight pressing upon me, and there were occasions when I thought my knees would buckle and I would fall to the ground never to rise again. I believe in retrospect this invisible weight was indeed the heavy hand of God upon my life, and later I found a passage of scripture that perfectly captured these ominous days of my life.

> For day and night your hand was heavy upon me; my strength was sapped as in the heat of summer. Then I acknowledged my sin to you and I did not cover up my iniquity. I said, "I will confess my transgressions to the LORD" — and you forgave the guilt of my sin. Psalm 32:4–5

In the context of these verses it is clear what God sought through the application of His heavy hand in the psalmist's life. He wanted David to stop hiding his iniquity, to acknowledge his sin, and to confess his transgressions. As the hound of heaven, He was in hot pursuit of David's heart, and He wanted David to come out from the bushes that he was hiding behind. As David resisted this difficult but divine invitation, God increased the intensity of His pursuit and attempted to bring David to bay through the increasing weight of His heavy hand. In a modern-day expression of these divine realities, I felt the hound of heaven was pursuing me, and though I understood what He was asking me to do, like David, I resisted the advances of my heavenly aggressor. Because of my fear of the light of exposure, I wasn't yet ready to surrender to His requirements. I continued to hold my head up, refusing to bow my neck in broken humility and submission. As the battle between us raged on for days, and I continued to resist the increasing conviction upon my soul, in a final convulsion of rebellion and in a vain attempt to throw off the shackles of God's authority in my life, I had one final infidelity with the woman I was involved with.

Immediately following this event, I felt overwhelmed with shame and conviction, and felt myself suffocating as the weight of God's hand seemed to push me under the swirling water I had been resisting for so long. In the same spirit of desperation with which Jonah cried out as the waves of God's severe mercy crashed over his head following his deliberate act of disobedience, something deep in my heart seemed to finally break and surrender as my soul cried out to God.

From inside the fish, Jonah prayed to the LORD his God. He said: "In my distress I called to the LORD, and he answered me. From the depths of the grave I called for help, and you listened to my cry. You hurled me into the deep, into the very heart of the seas, and the currents swirled about me; all your waves and breakers swept over me. I said, 'I have been banished from your sight; yet I will look again toward your holy temple.'" Jonah 2:1–4

The severe but loving mercy of God caused Jonah to cry out to the One he had been running from, and brought him to the place of confessing that he would once again look toward God's holy temple; thus signifying his turning back toward God. In much the same way, the handiwork of God's heavy hand finally accomplished its powerful and mysterious work in my own heart, as I collapsed in complete and glorious surrender to God. I knew I had to obey Him regardless of the impending consequences I had so feared, and I felt myself mysteriously drawn into the light of full exposure. As if by coincidence, I happened to have a luncheon appointment scheduled that very day with one of my pastors, and as we met, I felt compelled to confess to him the true depth of my struggle and sin.

Chapter 22

Confession

As we sat over lunch, I shared with my pastor, to the best of my ability at the time, the extent of the struggle in which I had been involved, and the depth of my failure. I say "to the best of my ability" because I'm sure I did not fully comprehend at the time the true depth of my sin or the scope of my bondage. In the years that followed, through an incredibly difficult and painful process that included extended periods of counseling, I slowly learned to face the true magnitude of the sin I tended to so easily minimize, and the extent of the bondage that reached as far back as my childhood. Nevertheless, I tried to convey to my pastor a sense of the ongoing battle in which I was entangled, and I confessed to him the primary manifestations of my failure, which included the one-time affair early in my marriage, the kiss that occurred between me and my sister-in-law, and the ongoing 5-year affair in which I was presently involved. I told him I knew I had a problem that was bigger than me, and that despite my best efforts to control it, I knew I would never be able to overcome it alone. I told him I desperately wanted help, that I was sick and tired of doing the wrong thing, and that I wanted to do the right thing by seeking the help I knew in my heart I so needed.

I chose my pastor as the first one to disclose my secret struggle to because I considered him my friend and I had a deep sense that he sincerely loved me and genuinely cared about my welfare. As I shared my story with him, including my shame, my fear, and my pain, he listened intently, and responded with love and sympathetic understanding. He tried to assure me that hope was not lost, that I could move forward in my life despite everything that had happened, and that God was big enough to do His part in healing my life and my marriage if I was willing to do my part in what would be necessary in the days ahead. He said he would talk to the other pastors, but he was confident they would recommend that Sheri and I begin meeting immediately with a professional counselor to whom they often referred people.

Although it was very difficult to confess to someone the dark and shameful things about myself that I had always tried to keep hidden, after speaking with my pastor I felt an immediate sense of both emotional and physical relief. It's as if a great weight was suddenly lifted off my shoulders, as God seemed to immediately bless the obedience He had so persistently and lovingly been requiring of me. I knew in my heart that I was no longer alone in my struggle. It wasn't just up to me to figure things out and to make things work. It wasn't just up to me to face my demons and find the strength to defeat them. I felt as if I had been alone in a battle — a battle in which I was seriously wounded, surrounded, and losing — and suddenly I had friendly reinforcements. I sensed that these reinforcements would be stronger and smarter than me; that they would know what to do and that they would be willing to fight on my behalf. I felt as if my allies would stand next to me under my overwhelming burden and assume much of the weight in order to give me some desperately needed relief.

After confessing and thus experiencing an unusual and almost immediate feeling of respite, I came to better understand in my heart the meaning of the following verses: "Brothers, if someone is caught in a sin, you who are spiritual should restore him gently. But watch yourself, or you also may be tempted. Carry each other's burdens, and in this way you will fulfill the law of Christ" (Galatians 6:1–2).

In the context of this passage, we are encouraged to bear one another's burdens, particularly as they relate to the power of specific sins that may have ensnared us as individuals. This passage of scripture is clear, and its truth was exhibited powerfully in my life through the ministry of a Christian friend who was willing to fulfill the law of Christ by hearing me and helping me to bear my burden. I sincerely believe confession is a powerful and significant step in the healing process. "Therefore confess your sins to each other and pray for each other so that you may be healed. The prayer of a righteous man is powerful and effective" (James 5:16).

I do not believe this means we should indiscriminately blab our sins to everyone and anyone who will listen, but I do believe it means we should be willing to confess our sins to a trusted friend and confidant who will then be willing to help us carry our burden, provide a level of accountability, and help us find the resources we might need in order to begin working toward freedom. I am convinced that one of the devil's most powerful and effective schemes is to isolate us in our battles through the fear of exposure, and deceive us into believing that the safest thing to do is to live a lie and continue crouching behind the bushes that hide our shame. Jesus said, "Then you will know the truth, and the truth will set you free" (John 8:32). It is the truth, and our willingness to face the truth and admit it not only to God, but also to one another, that will bring freedom from our bondages, thus serving as the basis of our renewed fellowship with God and with one another (I John 1:5–10).

I'm not sure I can explain exactly why, and I am not a theologian, but I do believe there is significant power in the confession of sin to one another. The Bible makes it clear that the Church is the body of Christ. It is made up of many members — a community of believers — that are interdependent on one another and desperately in need of each other[1]. There is no such thing as a "lone ranger" Christian, and none of us are strong enough or equipped to handle the enormity of life on our own. We need one another, and that's one reason God has designed the Church the way He has — as a body — and given us to one another. Again, I'm confident that one of the devil's greatest tactics to defeat our lives is to isolate us into fighting our toughest battles all alone. Because of his deception, and our natural inclination to hide our failures, we can easily convince ourselves that we have our sin under control and we are capable of managing our problem on our own, when in fact we are seriously in need of help from others. It's so easy to rationalize to ourselves, "I know I've been struggling with this area of my life, but I am really going to try hard, and I am going to get it together. I don't think I need to tell anybody else about it, because they probably wouldn't understand, and they would think less of me. Besides, I stand before God, and I answer to Him. I don't have to tell other people about my struggles."

Certainly there is a need to deal with our sin and our struggles privately before God as He works in our lives to make us more like Jesus, but that is one thing. It is quite another thing to continue struggling all alone with sinful patterns and bondages that have held us captive for years, and that have consistently defeated our lives over and over again. Sooner or later we must come to the place of admitting the truth and acknowledging that we are not in control of our sin, but that our sin is in control of us; that we have a serious problem that is really bigger than we have wanted to admit, and that we need someone else's help. My understanding is that, according to most twelve-step programs, this is the very first step necessary to the healing process: a person must be willing to admit to himself that he has a problem he cannot handle.

If you are struggling, like I was for so long, to find freedom from the sexual sin, or any other sin for that matter, that holds you captive, I beg you to please believe the truth, and to prayerfully consider finding a Christian friend — someone you respect and someone you can trust — and confessing your sin and your struggle to that person. The Christian church is a community of struggling believers, and we all desperately need one another. Do not continue to fight your battle alone. Do not continue to live a lie. Use wisdom and discretion, but realize you must move into the light if you want to break the power of sin in your life and find the true freedom God wants to give you. I wish I could tell you there is another way — an easier way — to find freedom, but there is not. I am convinced that confession is an indispensable and necessary step to real freedom, and that we must come to the place where we are willing to admit the truth to ourselves first, then to God, and then to another trusted person. Although the truth is an incredibly hard master to face when it calls our name and demands our obedience, it ultimately simplifies every struggle and makes freedom possible.

After confessing my struggle to my pastor, I knew I would have to then take the difficult step of confessing to my wife. That evening after the children went to bed, I asked Sheri if I could talk with her about something very important. I remember sitting in the great room of our home, and telling her the truth about who I really was, and the things I had been struggling with so deeply. I told her about the one-time affair early in our marriage, the kiss between her sister and I, and my ongoing affair with our close friend.

As Sheri listened, she responded immediately with a kind of stunned disbelief, and she thought I was joking. I had to tell her that the words I spoke were unfortunately true, and they were not a joke. I told her that I was tired of living the way I was living, that I was tired of the battle I had been fighting for so long, and I was tired of our failing marriage. I apologized for the things I had done wrong, said I was willing to submit completely to authority, that I had already confessed to our pastor earlier that day, and that I was willing to seek help by going to counseling. I said I would do anything to try to save our marriage if she was willing to fight for our marriage, and I told her I would submit to whatever she wanted me to do. If she wanted to divorce me, I said I would agree to the divorce, but that is not what I wanted. I told her if she wanted an arranged separation and wanted me to move out for a predetermined amount of time, that I would be willing to do so. I told her that if she no longer wanted to sleep with me, that I would understand, and I would sleep on the couch.

I'm sure my revelation and my words were like an unexpected bomb to Sheri, and as she realized their gravity, she seemed to respond with a kind of stunned numbness. As we continued to talk, we both began to cry, and Sheri told me she did not want to give up on our marriage. At one point she said that everything was really her fault, which of course wasn't true, and she said she was also willing to go to counseling to try to save our marriage. We then prayed together, and as we pleaded with God through the veil of our tears, we surrendered our marriage and our future back to Him. What was conspicuously absent from the entire scene was any sense of anger or rage, which Sheri had every right to feel given my confessions. Only many months later could Sheri begin to feel and express her offense, outrage, and anger toward me. This occurred by the grace of God, as He worked through her counseling process to slowly bring her wounded heart back to life.

---

1 The New Testament makes it clear that the Church is made up of many members who all need one another. The following is a list of several "one another" principles that we are exhorted to submit to in one another's lives:
  • Love one another — Romans 13:8; Galatians 5:3; I Thessalonians 3:12 and 4:9; I Peter 1:22; I John 3:11, 23 and 4:7, 11–13; II John 5
  • Be devoted to one another — Romans 12:10
  • Honor one another — Romans 12:10
  • Accept one another — Romans 15:7
  • Greet one another — Romans 16:16
  • Serve one another — Galatians 5:13
  • Care for one another — I Corinthians 12:25
  • Admonish one another — Romans 15:14
  • Bear one another's burdens — Galatians 6:2
  • Be kind to one another — Ephesians 4:32
  • Submit to one another — Ephesians 5:21
  • Confess your sins to one another — James 5:16
  • Show hospitality to one another — I Peter 4:9
  • Fellowship with one another — I John 1:17
  • Encourage one another — Hebrews 10:25
  • Build up (edify) one another — I Thessalonians 5:11
  • Exhort one another — Hebrews 3:13
  • We are members one of another — Romans 12:4–5
  • Forgive one another — Ephesians 4:32

CHAPTER 23

SUBMISSION TO AUTHORITY

When I had lunch with my pastor and made my confession, the other significant thing I told him was that I was willing to submit one-hundred percent to the authority of my pastors regarding my life and my marriage. Believing it is the model taught in the New Testament for the proper leadership of the Church, the church I was attending at the time had a plurality of pastors, and was therefore led through the combined giftedness and strengths of several men. I knew the pastor I was speaking with would share my predicament with the other pastors, and together they would recommend the direction they thought I should proceed given my arduous circumstances. I told him I was willing to submit to and accept any course of action my pastors recommended. If they thought I should go to counseling, I would. If they thought an arranged separation was best, and thought I should move out for a period of time, I would. If they thought I should read certain books or participate in a particular therapy group, I would. Of course, I had known these men for years and trusted their wisdom as well as their good hearts toward me and my family. It was not that I intended to unilaterally abdicate all control or responsibility for my life to these men, as if they would then be assuming the responsibility to formulate every decision on my behalf and determine my direction and future. Nor would it be their intention to commandeer my life by somehow forcibly seizing control and then pontificating to me their opinions and requiring my blind obedience regardless of my thoughts or feelings. My

115

116 STORIES: THE REDEMPTION of ONE MAN'S WOUNDED SEXUALITY

intuition simply told me the best thing I could do, given such circumstances, was to surrender and submit completely to the recommendation and guidance of the spiritual authorities God had placed in my life. I felt I had made such a complete mess of everything, and was so incapable of managing my problem alone, that the best thing I could do to start over and have any hope of rebuilding my life was to submit to the loving guidance of others more objective and wiser than me.

In retrospect, as I reflect on the slow, difficult, but redemptive process God began to take me through — a process that began on the day of my confession — I believe my willingness to submit from a broken heart of humility and destitution to the guidance of my spiritual authorities was significant to my healing process. My life was so shattered, and I was so overwhelmed with feelings of confusion, pain, and fear, that there was no way I could find the objective resources within myself that would be necessary to guide my life accordingly. A dying man going into surgery doesn't tell the doctor what to do, and a man lost at sea cannot find his way home. My circumstances were evidence enough that I was incapable of making right decisions, and proof that I needed others to help me and guide me. Although such dependence on others may appear as weakness in the world's eyes, I believe it is a strength when considered from the values of God's economy. In fact, I think my stubborn and autonomous heart, insistent on maintaining the illusion of control and demanding its own way for so many years, only proved to delay the healing process God could have begun so much earlier in my life. Since I depended so much upon myself and fought so hard to make my life work on my own terms, I delayed God's redemptive work in my life. It was only when I finally came to the end of myself — in large part due to the impossible circumstances I had created — that I recognized how desperately I needed others to help me. Only then God was finally able to move into my life and begin my healing process. I believe submission to authority was a great strength and blessing in my life — not a place of weakness, loss of control, or bondage — as the devil would lie to me and want me to believe.

The importance of submission to authority is taught over and over again throughout the Bible, and I was amazed when I took the time to do an extended study of the subject and see for myself the emphasis God places on this important principle. As I studied this several years ago when I was invited to teach on the subject at a men's retreat, I was astonished at what I found and eventually realized a notable connection between submission to authority and freedom from sexual bondage. While this important subject is worthy of its own book, I'll briefly share why I believe my submission to spiritual authority contributed so significantly to my healing process and eventual freedom.

As I studied, I learned that God has chosen to represent His own authority throughout the earth through an intricate system of God-instituted, delegated authorities. These ordained systems of God's authority include the home (Ephesians 5:21—6:4), the workplace (Ephesians 6:5–9), the society and government (Romans 13:1–7), and the Church (Hebrews 13:17; Acts 20:28; I Timothy 3:1–13). God established these systems of delegated authority in these various human institutions as a way of extending His divine authority throughout the entire earth and all of humanity.

Further, I saw that every human being is under these God-ordained systems of authority in one way or another, and is required by God to obey all such authorities in his life. Children, for example, are under the authority of their parents at home and their teachers at school. Women are under the authority of their husbands at home as well as the government that regulates society. Men are under the authority of their bosses at work, government officials, and the spiritual authorities of their church. No one is exempt from authority in his or her life, and submission to these God-ordained authorities is equivalent to submission to God Himself. To disobey God's established authority in our lives is to disobey God Himself! In any area of authority, God is displeased when there is disobedience or a heart of autonomy and rebellion. If a child disobeys his parents, God is displeased. In the same way, if a man disobeys his spiritual authority, God is displeased. Isn't it funny how we naturally expect a child to submit to his parents' authority, but we seem confused and unsure as we contemplate our submission as Christian men to our spiritual authorities at church?

In an alarming passage of scripture on the importance of biblical submission, which I believe is a dramatically understated teaching from God's Word in this day and age, we learn, through the prophet Samuel, of Saul's disobedience to God's clear instructions. In the surprising crescendo of this particular passage, Samuel severely rebukes Saul, and the sobering consequences of Saul's rebellion result in his rejection by God as king.

> But Samuel replied: "Does the LORD delight in burnt offerings and sacrifices as much as obeying the voice of the LORD? To obey is better than sacrifice, and to heed is better

than the fat of rams. For rebellion is like the sin of divination, and arrogance like the evil of idolatry. Because you have rejected the word of the LORD, he has rejected you as king." I Samuel 15:22–23

The holy prophet of God dares to compare rebellion to the sins of witchcraft and idolatry, so apparently the issues of submission and obedience are extraordinarily important to God!

Somehow, in a mystery, God's blessing and power follows submission to authority. A child is protected from the pouring rain as he walks alongside his father and stays under the protective covering of the father's umbrella. If the child chooses to rebel against his father, and run away, the child is no longer under the umbrella of the father's protection, and is now subject to the pouring rain and all possible consequences. The child will probably get soaking wet. The child might catch a cold, get pneumonia, and even die — all because he rejected the protective covering of his father's umbrella. That's kind of how spiritual authority works. As we move back into the place of submission to the God-ordained authorities in our lives, there is a God-ordained protection and approval that results, and God is then free to bless and work deeply in our lives. I believe this is why my submission to authority was so strategic to my healing process and eventual freedom. Submitting to my spiritual authorities was like submitting to God Himself. It was like coming in out of the rain. It was moving from a place of autonomy, duplicity, and darkness, to a place of dependence, truth, and light. It was God finally getting me in the place where He could begin to break the chains that had held me captive for so long.

Chapter 24
Therapy

As I expected, my pastors' immediate recommendation was that Sheri and I begin seeing a professional therapist. I believed in my heart God was going to lead me through the direction of my spiritual authorities, and since they thought therapy was the best thing for me, I agreed and complied immediately. I knew I needed serious help dealing with my issues, and I found the thought of meeting with someone who would be able to provide such assistance very appealing. After struggling alone with my problems for so long, and making such a total mess of my life, I welcomed the idea of inviting others to my side who would be able to contribute to my healing process. Like a drowning man drifting in the middle of the ocean, with powerful currents and waves crashing all around me, I had been thrashing about in the futile attempt to rescue myself for long enough. As I stepped into the light of exposure, I knew I desperately needed others to help me, and I guess I saw my therapist like a Coast Guard Marine equipped with life preservers and other life-saving equipment to facilitate my rescue.

When I started my therapy, I had no way of knowing it was going to be as involved as it ended up being, and I ultimately attended therapy with two different counselors for a total of almost 6 years. The first counselor was a professional therapist who worked with Sheri and I separately for 2 years and 7 months. He was one of the therapists we met with earlier in our marriage, but unfortunately I wasn't ready at that time to step completely into the light of truth, and I was less than honest with him regarding the true depth of my struggle. As a result, no significant progress was achieved during those earlier sessions, but I hoped this time would be different, and I promised him during our very first session that I would do my best to be completely honest on this go around. The second therapist was one of our pastors who has a graduate degree in counseling, and Sheri and I met with him together for 3 years and 2 months after I ended my sessions with the first therapist.

Although I believe my therapy was an indispensable part of my healing and freedom, it turned out to be a completely different process than I expected. As crazy as it sounds, I think the unexpected surprise of my therapy was that it ended up being so much about me. Although I knew I had an undeniable problem controlling my sexuality, at the time I easily dismissed my own responsibility and saw my wife and her unwillingness to have sex as the real problem. Her failure loomed so gigantic to me, I figured anyone else who looked at our lives would quickly conclude that she was the primary problem, and then go about the business of focusing more on her than me. Although I don't specifically remember thinking these very words, it was as if my heart justified itself with reasonings such as this: "Everyone knows a man needs to have sex, and everyone knows it's a woman's responsibility to satisfy her husband's sexual needs. Sheri refuses to have sex with me for prolonged periods of time, and she refuses to allow me to touch her, so what am I supposed to do? I can't help it if I'm a man and I have these sexual needs that have to be met. God knows and Sheri knows that I have a weakness in this area of my life, and if she would only have sex with me I would be all right. How can she deny me and then expect me not to fail in this area? I know that what I've done is wrong, but it's really her fault because if she would meet my needs as my wife, I would be satisfied and then I wouldn't struggle so deeply with controlling my sexuality."

Of course, although there was truth to the fact that my wife had deeply failed me in many ways, it was also true that I had deeply failed her in many ways, and I was wrongly focused on the speck in her eye while conveniently ignoring the beam in my own eye (Matthew 7:3–5). Consequently, in the same way a loving and wise parent forces his sick child to ingest medicine despite its terrible taste, my therapist had the difficult job of feeding me the distasteful medicine of self examination when I frequently and stubbornly refused to open my mouth — or heart — to his strange kindness.

I therefore think the greatest way my therapist contributed to my healing process was by helping me to slowly see and comprehend the much broader picture of my entire life, rather than focusing on just the smaller picture of my marriage. He helped me to see how I had arrived at the destination of my difficult marriage, and how my marriage didn't stand alone as an isolated circumstance in my life, but was in fact a depository for the culmination of all my life experiences and who I had become as a person. It's as if

I tended to see myself at number ten on an imaginary scale, and defined number ten as a marriage with a woman who wouldn't have sex with me. "That's my problem!" I thought. "I'm at number ten! I'm married to a woman who refuses to have sex with me!" And I focused on number ten and saw it as the problem in my life. What my therapist helped me discover was that "number ten" does not exist alone, but that to get to number ten, you must first go past number one, then number two, then number three, four, five, and so on. He helped me realize that my ultimate destination of number ten is only the natural conclusion and culmination of the path and direction I have already been walking. When I attended therapy, I intended to fix the precipitating problem of my marriage, and since I thought my wife was the primary problem with my marriage, I wrongly assumed the primary focus of the counseling would be directed toward "fixing" her. Imagine, therefore, my surprise when my therapist seemed more intent on talking about me and fixing me!

When I started my therapy I failed to comprehend the broader "story" of my life, and how the short stories I've shared throughout this book were like pieces of a puzzle that created the larger picture of who I really was as a man. Before my therapy, I had no idea how deeply I had been affected by so many influences in my life, like the magazines and books, the examples of masculinity provided by my father and my pastor, or the seductive women who had toyed with me. I saw those events as things that had happened to me years earlier, but had no real influence on the person I had become or the man to whom my wife was married. My therapist helped me with the difficult process of facing my past and comprehending how these things had deeply affected me as a person, had influenced the development of my sexuality, and had contributed to the kind of man I had become.

In the end I began to see that the healing I was seeking was not so much about my marriage, but it was more about who I was as a person and a man. It wasn't about the smaller picture of my marriage, but it was about the bigger picture of my entire life and who I was when my wife married me. It wasn't about focusing on "number ten" and trying to get it fixed, but it was more about contemplating numbers one through nine in my life, and considering how their cumulative effect had contributed to making my marriage what it was. It wasn't about getting my wife fixed so she would have sex with me, but it was about getting myself fixed and becoming a better man so my wife would hopefully *want* to have sex with me. Ultimately I learned that I had been asking the wrong questions for many years. I had been asking questions like, "What's wrong with my wife?" and "Why won't she have sex with me?" Only through my therapy process did I slowly learn to ask the right questions. Questions like, "What's wrong with me?" and "What is it about me as a man that makes it difficult for my wife to receive intimacy from me or to enjoy my touch?"

The other significant benefit that came out of my counseling process and contributed to my healing and freedom was the deep realization of my personal responsibility apart from the terrible things that had happened *to* me. I began to see in my heart that it's not so much what happens to you in life, but it's what you do with what happens to you that determines the kind of person you become. I began to see how deeply I had failed in this area of my life, and how I had used the difficulties of my life and marriage as an excuse to become an uglier person instead of a better person. It's true my wife couldn't respond to me and found it difficult to have sex with me, in large part because of wrong things alive in my heart — things that pushed her away from me rather than attracted her toward me. But rather than loving her unconditionally, I used her failure as an excuse to justify the horrible fruit that manifested itself in my life as a result — things like anger, bitterness, hatred, revenge, betrayal, duplicity, deceitfulness, and adultery. I was so quick to judge Sheri for the failure I detected in her life, but then allowed her failure to provoke terrible and heinous responses in my own life. My responses confirmed I was a horrible sinner and proved that I was far more guilty (beam) than the offenses I had so accurately detected in her life (speck).

In due course I realized that God was teaching me the essence of what it means to turn the other cheek (Matthew 5:38–42). What I had perceived as a "slap" from Sheri's hand (her rejection of me and refusal to have sex with me), provoked in me a counterattack in which I pounded her into the ground with the fist of my sinful responses. I thus proved that I was indeed the kind of man difficult for any woman to trust and enjoy. As I slowly, almost imperceptively, began to comprehend these lessons and realize the depth and ugliness of my own sin, it was as if I could hear the voice of God gently asking me, "Tony, are you willing to begin doing the right thing no matter what? Are you willing to love your wife unconditionally, even if she never has sex with you again? Are you willing to bear her slap, and not respond by pounding her back? Are you willing to turn the other cheek, and even if she continues to do the wrong thing and withhold herself from you, are you willing to respond in a way that is pleasing to me as your heavenly Father? Are you willing to stop using her sin as justification for your own sin?"

I knew I was hearing the voice of God, and as He gently prompted me to look more and more at the ugliness of my own sin, I began to slowly understand how deeply I had failed my wife, and as I did I could feel my sharp criticism and contempt toward Sheri begin to slowly drain away. I began to see that the main problem in my marriage wasn't Sheri, as I had always thought it was, but the main problem was me, and the kind of man I had been. I then realized that the counseling process was indeed more about me than it was about her, and God Himself was serious about doing business with me — business like helping me to see the truth and repent of my sexual bondage. God wanted me to recognize that many of the attitudes and expectations I had about sex in my marriage were wrong and didn't honor Him or my wife. God wanted to show me that He was big enough to heal my wife and my marriage if I was willing to first allow Him to begin my own desperately needed healing process.

CHAPTER 25

THE SMALL GROUP

As part of my counseling process, I was invited to become involved in a small group that consisted of several men who were all partic- ipating in therapy. The group was designed to provide support, encouragement, and accountability for each man as he slowly worked his way through his counseling process. In much the same way a greenhouse helps new plants to grow and become strong, the group provid- ed an environment that was conducive to growth and change as each man faced the often difficult process to which God had called him. Participating in this group allowed me to be part of a community of fellow strugglers, and my weekly involvement affirmed to me that I was not alone in my battle. There were other men who, like me, were wrestling deeply with issues such as facing their past, considering their wounded sexuality, contemplating and trying to understand their sin, and struggling with their difficult marriage. I was encouraged weekly by other men who could relate to my battle, and I drew strength from the group as we prayed for one another, shared our sto- ries and our lives with one another, and held one another accountable.

Central to our weekly meeting was a book by Dr. Dan Allender called *The Wounded Heart — Hope For Adult Victims Of Childhood Sexual Abuse.* Our format was to read a chapter in advance of our meeting, answer the chapter's corresponding questions in the accompanying study guide, and then come to the meeting prepared for discussion. Progress through the book was slow, and it wasn't unusual for us to spend many weeks on each chapter. In addition to the book itself, each man was given the opportunity to share his personal story with the rest of the group — an assignment that took many weeks by itself since there were several of us in the group. As we slowly read, discussed, and struggled our way through the book, I came to

125

recognize what I saw as two major sections. (Understand that the book itself is not literally divided into these two sections, but they represent my simplified way of relating to the material as we studied it.) The first section taught us about sexual abuse and the sad effects it has on people who have been victimized. I learned that sexual abuse creates a complicated web of confusing and conflicting influences that include strands like the following:

- Shame — If you know who I really am and what I really struggle with, you will look at me with disgust. You will think less of me, and you will reject me as a person.
- Contempt — I'm disgusted with myself because of how I am, and I will hate you if you see the truth about me.
- Helplessness — I cannot control my world or what happens to me. I am incompetent and inadequate.
- Lack of trust — I have already been deeply hurt by someone I trusted, so I will not allow myself to enjoy or trust others again. I will live at a safe distance from others.
- Ambivalence — I want intimacy with others but I am afraid of intimacy with others. I must be crazy.

The second section of Allender's book then taught us how the victim, once entangled in the strands of the web mentioned above, typically attempts to manage his life and his pain through an internal commitment to make life work on his own terms and through his own resources. The victim's doomed attempt to manage life despite the deep hurt and confusion within his heart inevitably affects his ability to maintain a healthy relationship with God or with others. This commitment to make life and relationships work on his own terms often leads to predictable symptoms, many of which I recognized at work in my own life. For me these included struggling with depression, suffering from sexual addiction, lacking true intimacy in relationships, failing to trust others, and adopting a manipulative style of relating in which I sought out relationships that met my needs and at the same time allowed me to protect myself from being hurt. I saw that I had the natural tendency in my relationships to be like a hungry bear trying to provide for himself. I tended to see other people like honey trees, and sensed that although they contained much that my heart longed for, they also had the power to hurt me. They contained the sweet and life-giving substance I sensed in my heart I needed to survive, but at the same time they could swarm me and deeply harm me with their "stings." Thus I learned from a very young age to approach others in a way that would allow me to get what I needed from them while not provoking them to attack.

Ultimately I slowly learned through *The Wounded Heart,* my group, and my therapy process that I could either continue to handle life my own way on my own terms, or I could surrender my autonomy and self-sufficiency and embrace God's path for my life (Proverbs 14:12; John 14:6). I saw that God's way was not necessarily going to be the easy way. It would require me to trust God in the "darkness" of my life rather than lighting the flaming torch of my own self-sufficiency in my attempt to survive (Isaiah 50:10–11). God's way would require a radical commitment to honesty, a willingness to face the truth, and the willingness to embrace and properly process the pain of my life instead of anesthetizing myself with drugs like workaholism, success, masturbation, denial, and anger. Ultimately, it would require my repentance, and like the prodigal son who came to his senses in the pigpen of life, God's way would require me to acknowledge my foolishness and my complete inability to manage my own life, and compel me to turn in humble and broken dependence back toward the Father.

In his book *Pure Desire,* pastor and author Ted Roberts conveys the importance of small groups to the healing process of sexual addiction. He says:

> One of the things I try to help these men see is that they can't be strong enough to win this war alone. They need God's help in their lives more now than ever. They need to fall into His arms as never before. And they need the help of men around them to fight the battle. Hell is treating them like pawns in order to tear at God's heart, and it is time they learned how to fight back with effectiveness...

> To do this effectively, we need a large team to help communicate in small group settings the reality of God's healing grace in families. Preaching plants the truth, but in small groups the truth begins to take root. The Church, as never before, has to become a healthy family for so many who have experienced unhealthy families and don't even realize it...

> These addicts must address their sense of worthlessness at the point of their shame. They have to find a safe place where

they can finally let all the secrets out — with nothing held back. Small group ministry is a critical key in this process. Without it we can never come to the place of confessing our sins to one another in order to be healed (see Jas. 5:16)[1]

I agree with Roberts' observations, and believe involvement with my small group was strategic to my own healing process. I think this was true because at times I felt like an alien who had landed on a strange planet. Think of it. If an alien from another world somehow found himself on Earth, he would probably be confused, disoriented, and overwhelmed. He would have so much to learn because everything would be so new. He would have no idea how to operate a door, sit on a chair, or put shoes on or take them off. He wouldn't know how to use a comb, drive a car, or speak this strange new language. He'd have so much to learn, and that's kind of how I felt as I began easing into the new world of honesty and repentance.

Since I felt like I had landed on a new planet, I had to learn how to function accordingly. Even if it hurt, I had to learn how to be honest with myself. I had to learn to recognize my sinful tendencies in the way I related to others. I had to learn to feel my own heart, and how to give and receive intimacy in my relationships. Instead of asking wrong ones, I had to learn to ask the right questions, and how to trust God more than ever before. I had to learn what to do with my pain when I could no longer medicate it with things like Baby Ruths and masturbation. I had to learn what it meant to humble myself, and how to wait on God in the darkness, and what it meant to journey back toward my Father's heart. The laws that governed the new kingdom in which I had landed were foreign to me, and I had to learn to speak the language of the King. Of course, these are all lessons I am still slowly learning, but my small group was instrumental in helping me begin my new journey. As the men in my group met weekly, we were more often than not clumsy and awkward in our abilities to share our struggles with one another, but we had each landed in this strange new world, and with wide-eyed wonder our journeys had begun.

---

1 *Pure Desire,* Ted Roberts, Regal Books, 1999, pages 39, 59, and 74.

CHAPTER 26

THE VOW

Several months into my counseling process, my therapist and I were talking about repentance. As I turned to face my past and attempted to understand the person I had become and my sinful behavior, I began to contemplate deeply what true repentance would look like in my life. Why was I attracted to the sinful patterns in my life that I seemed to turn to so often, like a dog turning to eat his own vomit? Why did these sinful tendencies hold so much power over me, and why did they control me? How could I break these powers in my life, and how would I know that I was really free? What would true repentance look like in my life, how would I know if I was really repentant, and how would the people around me know that I was really a repentant man? As we reflected on these important questions over a period of weeks, my therapist suggested one day that I consider talking to some other men about the topic. He recommended that I choose several men I respected and considered godly, and then talk to them about their thoughts on the matter. I thought this idea was excellent, and I decided to pursue the assignment in the hope of finding clarity through the combined wisdom of several godly men. I created the following brief questionnaire and over the next 5 weeks discussed it with nine of my Christian friends:

- What is repentance?
- Is repentance important in the life of a Christian?
- What should a Christian do in order to experience true repentance?
- How does a Christian know if he has experienced true repentance?
- What other thoughts or comments do you have on this subject?

Although each interview was interesting and helpful, one particular meeting became what I would later call a "divine appointment."

129

This particular meeting was with the pastor of a large and well-known church in the St. Louis area, and although I did not know him very well personally, I did respect him from a distance and thought he would be a good person to talk with. As we sat down for lunch, we began our discussion, and I introduced him to my questionnaire. I explained to him that I was in therapy dealing with my marriage and other issues in my life, and as part of my process I was interviewing respected Christian friends on the topic of repentance. He immediately responded by telling me he would be glad to answer my questions to the best of his ability, but he inquired further and wondered if I would be willing to share with him what was really going on in my life, and what was really behind the purpose of the survey. I therefore proceeded to share my story with him, and as he listened intently, I disclosed to him to the best of my ability an overview of my life and my marriage, and how I ended up in therapy. I didn't hide anything from him, and I confessed the details of my ever-present battle with my sexuality, the depth of my moral failure, and the struggle of my difficult marriage.

As he listened carefully to my story, he interrupted me at one point near the end, and said he had a question for me. I invited his question, and he asked me about masturbation. "Tony, I know you have struggled with masturbation in your past, but how are you doing with it now? Are you continuing to masturbate at this time in your life?" I responded by confessing — with a sense of embarrassment and shame — that I was continuing to masturbate, but I really didn't see any alternative because of my marital difficulties. My wife didn't have sex with me for prolonged periods that usually consisted of many months, and I figured masturbating was at least better than committing adultery. As he inquired further about the practice of masturbation in my life, I shared with him about my lifelong struggle with the issue. I told him about finding my father's pornography when I was a boy, and how I started masturbating at a very young age. As he listened carefully to my story, he said he wanted to challenge me regarding this issue in my life, and said he had some things he wanted to share with me.

He then shared what he believed was God's design and purpose for the expression of sexuality within the God-ordained parameters of marriage. He said he believed the Bible teaches that we are to honor God and honor our wives with our sexuality. He said that my sexuality is really a gift that God has given exclusively to my wife through the vessel of my body, and that likewise, her sexuality is a gift that God has given exclusively to me through the vessel of her body. As he shared these things with me I envisioned a

Christmas gift, and I realized using my sexuality for my own pleasure would be like secretly opening someone else's Christmas gift when he or she wasn't around. He said that my wife is the only one who has the right to my sexuality; it belongs to her and to no one else, and to express it apart from her would be wrong because it is not God's design. He continued by explaining that it would be wrong in God's eyes for me to ever express my sexuality in any way apart from my wife, including looking at pornography, having an affair, or even masturbating. Such activities would be wrong he said, because I would be opening the gift of my sexuality for my own pleasure, apart from my wife.

He then asked me to consider these ideas, and asked if I would be willing to pray about completely surrendering my body, my penis, and my sexuality to God in a new way. He asked me to pray about making a pledge to honor both God and my wife with my sexuality, which would mean I could never again express my sexuality in any way, including masturbation, apart from my wife.

I had never heard such an idea in my life, and although something deep in my heart was wooed by the depth of these thoughts and words, I immediately objected and told him I thought such a standard would be impractical for me to maintain, especially given my impossible marital circumstances. I pleaded, "Pastor, you don't understand what my life is like! My wife won't have sex with me! For months and months I am not allowed to touch her. If I surrendered my sexuality to my wife alone, then my sexuality would never be expressed because she almost never wants it. What will I do? How can I possibly die so completely to myself to make such a thing possible?" Despite my desperate questions and my obvious sense of being completely overwhelmed by what he said, my Christian friend was unyielding in his difficult challenge, and he answered me without apology. "Tony, you can't do it! It will be impossible for you, and that's why you will have to cast yourself so completely on God's grace, and depend on Him more desperately every day than you ever have in your entire life. You will need His help and His grace, every day, every hour, every moment! If He does not help you, then you will not be helped. But I believe that if you make this decision, and if you surrender your sexuality to God from a broken and desperate heart, that He will keep his end of the bargain. I'm not saying it will be easy, but He is a big God, and He can give you victory!"

As we continued to talk, my heart began to see a kind of vision, and although I did not share it with my pastor friend, I sensed it was a kind of strange gift from God. As my pastor friend was talking with me, I saw myself in a vast and hot desert. In this vision I was single. I was being called to a journey, and as I was about to begin my journey, God placed around my neck a vessel of cool and clean water. I realized I would need this life-giving provision of water to sustain me as I faced the difficult journey ahead, but then I heard the voice of God instructing me. He told me that the vessel of water was not for me. He told me it was His provision for someone else — someone I was to find along my way. He said that He saw this one in the desert also, and that she would be thirsty when I found her. He said that He was sending me to her, and He was trusting me with the stewardship of delivering to her the cool water I carried around my neck. He said that when I found her, she would also be carrying a vessel of water, and that her vessel would have my name written on it. He said that we would be very thirsty along the journey, but He wanted us to wait for one another to drink. He promised that when we found one another we could drink deeply from the vessel provided to us in one another, and He was trusting us to wait for one another.

As I understood the meaning of this beautiful vision, my heart began to break as I realized how deeply I had failed in the stewardship God had entrusted to me. I knew that I had started my journey long ago, and that all along the way I had failed to protect the vessel God had placed around my neck — the vessel of my sexuality, which God intended as a gift for me to deliver to my wife. Rather than protecting this precious vessel, and saving it for the one to whom it belonged, I began opening it early in my journey, giving it away to others, and spilling it all along the ground — wasting it. I realized how deeply I had failed God, and how deeply I had failed my wife. Tears began streaming down my face as I realized my failure, and I felt overwhelmed with a sense of loss because of what I had done.

But then, in a mystery, it was as if I could sense the presence of God inviting me through the words of my Christian friend. He was telling me that God is the God of grace, and the God of second chances. I could sense that God was inviting me to a new beginning, and He was willing to place a new vessel around my neck, with a fresh supply of cool and clean water. I sensed that the place I was standing was somehow a holy place, and that mystically this had become a powerful and holy moment in my life. Like Moses at the burning bush, I could hear the voice of God calling me through a holy fire, and like Moses, I knew I could not do the thing He was asking me to do. I asked my friend if he would pray over me, and as he began to pray my heart seemed to break deeper than ever before. With my usually stiff neck now broken in sorrow, I bowed my head in submission to God to match the stature of my broken heart, and I symbolically took off my shoes in reverence of the holy ground on which I was standing.

As the pastor finished his prayer, he told me he would be a witness of my vow before God if I was ready to make such a commitment. He said that I should see a kind of altar in my mind's eye, and that I should put my body, my penis, and my sexuality on the altar of sacrifice to God. I knew I was in the very presence of God, and I knew what He was asking of me. I began to pray through my tears, and I cried out for God to save me. I began confessing my sin and my failure to God, and I told God that I wanted to do what I had never done in my entire life. I told Him I wanted to honor Him and honor my wife with my sexuality. I told Him I wanted to do the right thing, and that I wanted to surrender my sexuality and my body to Him. I told Him I wanted to save myself for my wife, and that I never wanted to express my sexuality apart from her again. But even as I prayed, my heart broke even deeper because I knew the complete impossibility of my pledge, and my heart seemed to groan as I cried out in desperation, because I knew I could not do such a thing. I told God that I wanted to make this vow, but I was afraid that I would fail. I begged Him to do for me what I could not do for myself, and I pleaded for His mercy and grace. I pictured in my mind an altar of sacrifice, and I pictured myself placing my body, my penis, and my sexuality on the altar. As I did this, I knew these things that had been the center of my life for so long no longer belonged to me; they belonged to God, and I would have to trust Him completely. In that moment, I surrendered these parts of my life to Him, and I promised God that I would honor Him and honor my wife from then on, by His grace, to the best of my ability. It was another significant moment of glorious defeat on the difficult path I was traveling, and I would later come to recognize this event as one of the most important and sacred of my life. As I thanked my pastor friend for his love and ministry in my life, I felt a strange sense of ambivalence. While I was assured that God had met with me in a special way, I was cautiously suspicious of what my vow would mean to my life in the days ahead. Little did I know that there would still be many challenging days to come.

CHAPTER 27

EMBRACING PAIN
& PSALM 131

After making my vow, something began to change, but it wasn't the change I would have hoped for. Most of the time it seemed as if Sheri and I were living separate lives. We attended counseling apart from one another, and the cold distance that separated our hearts and our bodies remained. I remember so many nights when we went to bed, and although she was only a foot or two away, it felt like a million miles separated us. Sometimes it felt like torture to lay there next to her in the darkness. I would hear the rhythm of her breathing change as she quickly fell asleep, and then wonder how she could sleep so easily when I was in so much pain right next to her. She seemed completely oblivious and unconcerned about my pain, and I wondered at times if she had any idea who I was or what I felt inside. As I struggled deeply with the invisible wall that lived between us, my mind frequently raced between thoughts and feelings of depression, anger, self-contempt, rage, heartache, and grief. In the darkness, wide awake, listening to the slow and rhythmic sound of Sheri's breathing, I knew on such nights that sleep would still be hours away for me, and it was on such nights I came to recognize my own bleeding soul.

I knew that if I somehow cut or slashed my physical body that blood would gush from the wound, and that picture seemed to help me understand what I was feeling in my soul. It was as if something deep inside of me had been slashed open, and I could feel my soul hemorrhaging as it oozed my inner pain and poison. At times an invisible weight seemed to descend

135

upon me, and as it settled on my chest and seemed to push me into the bed, I literally gasped for air as I found it almost impossible to breathe. On such dark nights I was haunted by the remembrance of the passage I had found earlier in Isaiah.

> Let him who walks in the dark, who has no light, trust in the name of the LORD and rely on his God. But now, all you who light fires and provide yourselves with flaming torches, go, walk in the light of your fires and of the torches you have set ablaze. This is what you shall receive from my hand: You will lie down in torment. Isaiah 50:10–11

I knew this strange promise was being fulfilled in my life on these horrible nights, and I understood what it meant to lie down in torment. At times I struggled with God as I tried to understand what He wanted from me, and at other times I tried to push Him away in a desperate attempt to make Him leave me alone. I longed for a quiet place of peace and respite for my troubled soul, but was incapable of finding it with my bleeding pain as my constant companion. I knew the passage in Isaiah was inviting me to submit to the darkness that surrounded me, and to trust in the Lord in the midst of the darkness rather than lighting the torch of self-sufficiency in an attempt to deliver myself. God, it seems, was asking me to do the one thing that would be most difficult for me to do — He was asking me to do nothing; to accept the darkness He was allowing in my life; to sit quietly in the shadows; to wait on Him and to trust in Him; and to not light my own torch or fire in an attempt to find my own way out of the darkness. As I slowly understood what God was asking of me, I at first cringed with a kind of horrified disbelief, and complained that He might as well be asking me to speak Chinese! I felt that He was requiring something of me that I was completely incapable of giving, and that His very asking this of me was profoundly unfair. Yet, despite my resistance to His requirement, the continuous pain of my bleeding soul and frequent nights of torment were almost constant reminders that I had no other alternative, and I slowly began to learn the strange lesson of what it means to embrace pain and to trust God in the darkness.

I had an image in my mind, which I believe the Lord had given me, that helped me understand what He was asking of me. I saw the image of a hot stove. I knew that if I was to somehow accidentally place my hand on a hot stove, that I would instantly feel the pain, and everything in my being would scream at me to immediately remove my hand from the source of pain. This would be the natural and understandable reaction to such a situation, and this image illustrated how I had lived my life. Whenever something happened that caused me pain, I would quickly respond by doing everything and anything possible to eliminate the pain. These actions of self-protection and preservation included the following: lighting torches such as talking, convincing, and persuading in the attempt to manipulate the painful situation in my favor; using various emotions and techniques like anger, rage, avoidance, denial, or silence to keep the pain as far away from me as possible; and using various compulsions and addictions like masturbation, food, workaholism, busyness, and entertainment in the attempt to distract and anesthetize myself from the pain in my life. What I began to see and understand was that God was inviting me to forsake my own idolatrous way of dealing with the pain in my life. "Then you will defile your idols overlaid with silver and your images covered with gold; you will throw them away like a menstrual cloth and say to them, 'Away with you!'" (Isaiah 30:22). He was inviting me to instead submit to the peculiar way He wanted me to process my pain. Rather than employing the natural reaction of yanking myself away from the source of pain, He was inviting me to submit to its presence. Rather than running away from the pain, He was inviting me to move toward it. Rather than lighting torches of self-sufficiency, He was inviting me to humbly trust in Him as I quietly sat in the darkness. Rather than protecting myself from pain through medication and addiction, He was inviting me — although I didn't understand how or why — to embrace the pain as my closest friend.

> ...For my soul is full of trouble and my life draws near the grave. I am counted among those who go down to the pit; I am like a man without strength...You have put me in the lowest pit, in the darkest depths. Your wrath lies heavily upon me; you have overwhelmed me with all your waves...I am confined and cannot escape; my eyes are dim with grief... Why, O LORD, do you reject me and hide your face from me? From my youth I have been afflicted and close to death; I have suffered your terrors and am in despair. Your wrath has swept over me; your terrors have destroyed me. All day long they surround me like a flood; they have completely engulfed me. You have taken my companions and loved ones

from me; the darkness is my closest friend. Selections from
Psalm 88

I could sense that God had brought me to this place of darkness and
pain, and He was asking me to submit to it in humble obedience while I
waited and trusted in Him.

> The LORD is good to those whose hope is in Him, to the
> one who seeks Him; it is good to wait quietly for the
> salvation of the LORD. It is good for a man to bear the yoke
> while he is young. Let Him sit alone in silence, for the
> LORD has laid it on Him. Let him bury His face in the dust
> — there may yet be hope. Let Him offer his cheek to one
> who would strike him, and let him be filled with disgrace.
> For men are not cast off by the Lord forever. Though he
> brings grief, He will show compassion, so great is his
> unfailing love. For He does not willingly bring affliction or
> grief to the children of men. Lamentations 3:25–33

I knew the gospel wasn't an abstract idea I believed only in my head, but
that it was a living message that God was applying directly to my life. There
was a very real crucifixion happening as God was killing something in my
soul that He knew had to die before I could experience the life of God res-
urrected within me.

It was at this time — while learning what it means to embrace pain —
that the Lord allowed me to find Psalm 131. It became my favorite scripture
at the time, and continues to be my favorite to this very day. I give this short
Psalm — only three verses — the credit of literally saving my life. When I
was so discouraged I wasn't even sure I wanted to live, I found these verses,
and like a life preserver, they gave me something to hold on to and they
helped me to hold my head above the tumultuous and dark waters that
swirled around me.

> My heart is not proud, O LORD, my eyes are not haughty;
> I do not concern myself with great matters or things too
> wonderful for me. But I have stilled and quieted my soul;
> like a weaned child with its mother, like a weaned child is my
> soul within me. O Israel, put your hope in the LORD both
> now and forevermore. Psalm 131

Like a stick of dynamite, which appears deceptively small, this short Psalm is loaded with far more power than its undersized package would indicate. As I read the words, verse two leapt off the page, and I knew in my heart that it was what I wanted and desperately needed in my life — to still and quiet my soul like a weaned child. I thought that sounded great, and I wondered how I could capture the romantic essence of these words and make them the reality of my life. And so my heart broke as I cried out to God and begged Him to help me make these words real in my life. "How, oh God? How do I still and quiet my soul? That sounds so wonderful God, but I do not know how to do it!" Fueled by a kind of desperation to find the place of stillness, quiet, peace, and respite I was so hungry for, I began to read, study, memorize, and meditate upon this Psalm for a period of time that transpired from days to weeks, and then from weeks to months.

In the same strange way a cow draws life-giving nutrition as it slowly chews its cud, I mysteriously began to draw life from these precious words of God as I meditated upon them day after day. I learned from *Strong's Concordance* that the word "concern" used in verse one means to walk a path carrying a heavy weight. I knew that this word accurately described my life, and I felt worn out from walking such a long path, for such a long time, with such a heavy weight. I longed for God to deliver me from carrying the heavy burdens of my life, and wondered what it would be like to walk the path of life unencumbered in such a way. Further, I learned from *Strong's* that the word "great" used in verse one means something that is twisted, like a thread or a tassel, and the word "wonderful" means something that is great, difficult, hard, hidden, marvelous, or wondrous. As I continued to meditate upon these things, I came to see a clear distinction between two different ways I could choose to live my life. I could demonstrate a heart of pride, autonomy, and self-sufficiency by walking through my life carrying the weight of its difficult and twisted nature, or I could still and quiet my soul like a weaned child with its mother. I saw two different images that helped me to understand the distinction. The first image was one of a fisherman who tangled his fishing line into a huge bird's nest of a mess. He's a nervous wreck as he focuses on the chaos he has created and impatiently tries to solve his own problem by futilely attempting to eliminate his twisted mess. The other picture was that of a small baby — still and quiet — content to be close to its mother. One was an image of chaos, the other was an image of peace. One was an image of noise, the other was an image of quiet. One depicted how my life had been for so long, and one illustrated how I wanted my life to be. As I reflected on such thoughts, it's as though I could sense the gentle voice of God inviting me: "Tony, will you trust in Me? Will you lay down your pride and your haughty eyes? Will you stop walking the path carrying the weight of trying to straighten out your twisted and difficult life? Will you stop asking so many questions and insisting on the answers? Will you still and quiet your noisy soul before Me? Will you wait for Me? Will you stop lighting your own torches and stop trying to make your own way out of the darkness? Tony, will you stop dealing with your pain from your own resources? Will you embrace the pain I am allowing you to go through, and will you trust in Me?"

It was through such difficult days that I slowly began to learn what it means to embrace the pain of life and to trust God in the darkness. I wanted God to remove all my problems, and knew that I could trust Him if He would do so. But God wanted me to trust in Him first, and learn to be content with His presence in my life — like a weaned baby with its mother — regardless of the circumstances or darkness that surrounded me.

CHAPTER 28

Physical Pain & a Taste of Freedom

Weeks and then months began to pass as I slowly learned what it meant to still and quiet my soul like a weaned child with its mother, to embrace pain as my closest friend, and to trust in the Name of the Lord as I walked through the darkness with no light. These were lessons that were not easy for me to learn, and lessons that were completely foreign to all of my natural instincts and impulses. Although these days were incredibly difficult and lonely, I took comfort in the secure knowledge that I was a child of God, evidenced by His clear hand of discipline and training in my life.

> Our fathers disciplined us for a little while as they thought best; but God disciplines us for our good, that we may share in His holiness. No discipline seems pleasant at the time, but painful. Later on, however, it produces a harvest of righteousness and peace for those who have been trained by it. Therefore, strengthen your feeble arms and weak knees. Make level paths for your feet, so that the lame may not be disabled, but rather healed. Hebrews 12:10–13

The pain that became my familiar companion during these difficult days not only included the spiritual pain of God's discipline in my life, the emotional pain of my strained and lonely marriage, but also the very real physical pain of my body as it violently rebelled against the complete absence of sex-

141

ual release. I am not a medical doctor, so I cannot explain exactly what happened, but I know my body threw an absolute fit as it protested the level of abstinence my vow to God required. I've never been very good at depriving my body; for example, I've never fasted successfully because it seems like every fiber of my body screams at me, "What are you doing? Feed me! I am hungry and I demand to be satisfied right now! Are you nuts? How dare you try to deprive me of food! Eat, and eat something quick!" It has always been difficult to hold my raging flesh at bay, as it demands and tries to force me to serve it. In much the same way, my body began to quickly rebel when I made my vow depriving it of any kind of sexual release.

Within days of my vow, my testicles were incredibly sore and swollen, and produced a pain that was so intense it frequently radiated into my lower abdomen and made it very uncomfortable for me to stand and move about. This physical pain became my constant companion and, like the tip of an iceberg visible above the surface of the water, became my most obvious reminder of my battle. Although an occasional wet dream provided a brief respite, the pain would quickly return along with the accompanying sense of misery. In addition to occasional wet dreams, semen almost continuously leaked from my body. At times there was a kind of seepage that occurred throughout the day, but more often than not there was a discharge when I urinated. It's as though my body needed some relief from the constant pressure it was under and simply chose to slowly eliminate fluid in this way. I can only imagine that my body had been accustomed to a certain cycle of release — a kind of sexual rhythm — that began when I was just a boy. Over the years, I masturbated frequently, and learned to serve my body in this way whenever it called to me. When my vow required me to suddenly take control of my body, my body responded with a fit of violence and rebellion. I was experiencing a kind of physical withdrawal, in much the same way a drug addict might, as I began to break the sexual addiction I had always served.

It was during this profoundly difficult period of my life that insult was added to injury, and I suffered a kidney stone attack. It was without a doubt, far and away, the most intense and violent physical pain I have ever suffered. I remember literally laying on the family room floor, curled up in a fetal position, crying like a baby because the pain was so unbearable. I was unable to pass the kidney stone, so I had to have surgery. As part of my surgery the doctor had to place a stint inside my body between my kidney and my bladder. He later explained that because of the trauma of surgery, the

PHYSICAL PAIN & A TASTE OF FREEDOM   143

delicate tube — about the size of a pencil lead — from which he had removed the kidney stone would swell shut and cause more pain than the stone itself. He said he would leave the stint in for about a week, which would allow my kidneys and bladder to function properly, and he would then have to manually remove the stint through, of all places, my penis! HOLY SMOKES!

I'm still not sure which was worse: the kidney stone itself, or the week that followed. Every time I urinated, the pain was unbearable and it seemed like I was passing more blood than urine. Then there was the torture of waiting and anticipating the dreaded day of the stint removal, and the absolute horror of the event itself. Imagine, if you can, a huge stainless steel instrument, consisting of a rod strong enough to insert a camera for the doctor's use, and a claw designed to capture the stint. Then imagine the doctor inserting the entire beast of an instrument through the end of your penis, from the outside in, pushing it around until he finds what he's after, and then pulling the entire contraption, along with the 8-inch stint itself, back out through the penis! To make matters worse, imagine the doctor unable to accomplish his goal and therefore removing the entire apparatus, and then starting over by reinserting the giant contraption and trying again! It was without a doubt one of my worst experiences ever.

It seemed that the timing of this entire episode could not have been worse, but as I was in the hospital, the Lord spoke to me through it all. I felt as though I heard the quiet voice of God showing me that what was happening to my physical body was an outward manifestation of the surgery that God Himself was accomplishing in my soul. It's as though He said to me, "Tony, in the same way something went wrong with your physical body, something that has caused you enormous pain and suffering and had to be removed through, of all places, your penis, I am now operating on you spiritually. There is another thing in you that went wrong, something related to your sexuality and your penis, and through this dark valley of suffering and pain, I as the Master Surgeon am removing it from your life. Will you continue to submit to Me in the same way you have submitted to this physical doctor, and will you allow Me to remove from you the thing that has caused you so much pain?" It was a powerful experience for me to sense God's presence in such a dark valley, and I bowed my head before Him again as I attempted to submit my life to His control and direction. Rather than rebelling against my emotional and physical pain, I welcomed them to the best of my ability.

Many months had passed since the day I made my vow, and although nothing seemed to be changing outwardly in the circumstances of my marriage, something happened one day that revealed to me that God was slowly, almost imperceptively, changing something on the inside of me, and I experienced my first taste of true freedom from the sexual bondage that had held me captive for so long. One day, my boys wanted me to take them to the neighborhood public swimming pool. After arriving at the pool, I sat on a lounge chair on the pool deck and passed the time reading a book and enjoying the warm sunshine as my boys played in the water. I occasionally looked up to see my boys splashing and romping, and as I looked up one time, I quickly noticed, right in front of me, a beautiful girl wearing a skimpy bikini. I couldn't help but notice her, and as I began to follow her with my eyes, I immediately caught myself and realized what I was doing, and I brought my eyes back to the book I had been reading. I thought to myself, "That's the last thing I need to be looking at!"

I continued to read and suddenly something occurred to me. I looked up, and as I looked all around me, I realized I was surrounded by bikinis! There were numerous attractive girls all around me, and most of them were wearing provocative swimming suits. When I realized this, it occurred to me that I was in the midst of all these beautiful girls in skimpy bikinis, and I had not even noticed! As these thoughts rushed at me, something happened to me that is very hard to describe. I literally felt the Holy Spirit leap with joy within me, and I can only imagine it was the same way He caused the baby in Elizabeth's womb to leap when Mary visited her (Luke 1:39–41). I couldn't believe I had been in that environment, and I hadn't even noticed all those beautiful and scantily clad girls. As I realized this was a significant and holy event for me, it's as if I heard the voice of God rejoicing over me and with me in that precious moment. "See, Tony! I am God! I am giving you the victory! I am doing for you what you could never do for yourself! I am setting you free! I am breaking the chains, and I am giving you a new heart!" It was one of the most powerful and glorious moments of my life, and although there would still be difficult days ahead, this event represented my first taste of true freedom and victory.

> The LORD your God is with you, he is mighty to save. He will take great delight in you, he will quiet you with his love, he will rejoice over you with singing. Zephaniah 3:17

Physical Pain & a Taste of Freedom 145

I will go before you and will level the mountains; I will break down gates of bronze and cut through bars of iron. I will give you the treasures of darkness, riches stored in secret places, so that you may know that I am the LORD, the God of Israel, who summons you by name. Isaiah 45:2–3

Chapter 29

Two Steps Forward & One Step Back

Sheri and I continued to attend counseling separately, and as the months passed, I was soon approaching the 2-year anniversary of successfully honoring my vow. Those 2 years were without a doubt among the most difficult years of my life, and as I continued to struggle with the reality of my disastrous marriage, and the reality of the unrelenting physical pain that had become my constant companion, it seemed as if there was no light at the end of the tunnel. At times I felt overwhelmed with grief and depression, and I despaired of life itself. I frequently struggled with thoughts of divorce and suicide, and wondered to myself how much longer I could wait for a God who didn't seem interested in my life or pain, and certainly didn't seem like He was in any big hurry to rescue me or my marriage. At such tumultuous times my emotional life most resembled the path of a screaming roller coaster, and I felt like I was barely holding on for dear life. I wanted to trust in God, and I wanted to still and quiet my soul before Him like a weaned child with its mother, but at times the darkness that engulfed me, and the pain that swirled through my soul and body were so overwhelming that I lost all hope and simply wanted to give up.

How long, O LORD? Will you forget me forever? How long will you hide your face from me? How long must I wrestle with my thoughts and every day have sorrow in my heart? How long will my enemy triumph over me? Look on me and answer, O LORD my God. Give light to my eyes, or I will sleep in death. Psalm 13:1–3

It was during this time of hopeless despair that I began to crash and burn in my relationship with my therapist. By this time I had been meeting with him for about 2 years, and was utterly frustrated with the direction and progress of our time together. In view of the horrible situation at home between me and my wife, I was desperate in my desire to discuss my marriage. I felt that we should be focusing on the marriage, and that after 2 years of counseling, it was time for Sheri and I to begin meeting together and start dealing head-on with the marriage itself. I continued to struggle deeply with the issue of sex in my marriage, or better said, the lack of sex in my marriage, and felt at times that I was going to go absolutely insane if I was required to continue living with no sex in my life. I understood that Sheri had many difficult wounds she was slowly working through, many of which were delivered by my own terrible actions as I had failed her deeply in many ways, and I further understood there were many issues that I had to continue dealing with in my own heart and life, such as my difficult relationship with my father, my troubled sexual development and abuse, my own sexual addiction and tendency to use sex to medicate my troubled soul, and my tendencies to use my style of relating to control and manipulate the people and circumstances around me. We had been exploring all these issues in my life for the past 2 years, and I was willing to continue talking about them, but I had a growing conviction that it was also time to start meeting with Sheri in therapy and dealing with the marriage itself. My therapist totally disagreed with my assessment of the situation, and although he wouldn't explain the basis of his reasoning, he made it clear to me in no uncertain terms that he would not meet with my wife and I together.

In view of this disagreement, I sought advice from one of my pastors. I was committed to the principle of submission to spiritual authority in my life, and appealed to him for his insight. After expressing my concerns to him regarding the situation, my pastor seemed to agree that it was time for Sheri and I to meet together for marriage counseling. He said that he would be willing to personally come along and sit in on my sessions for a period of time to note progress, and said he would talk with the therapist and make sure we began meeting with my wife in the near future. I deeply appreciated the love, concern, and commitment my pastor demonstrated for my life by his willingness to help me in such a fashion. We began meeting together for breakfast every Tuesday morning, and then attending sessions together. As the weeks and then months passed, the three of us continued dealing with the various issues in my life, and my wife also continued to see the therapist on her own, separately from me. After another 6 months had passed, I began requesting again that we begin meeting with my wife and dealing with our marital issues. My therapist again made it clear that he would not meet with my wife and I together, because he did not believe it was the right time. I tried to convey to him the impossibility of our circumstances and life at home. I told him I would even be willing to meet with him two times a week — one time by myself, but the other time with my wife — and tried to convey that I just wasn't sure I could continue to hang in there for much longer given the difficult circumstances with no end or hope in sight. He responded by telling me I was free to quit meeting with him if that's what I felt I had to do, but that he would not meet with my wife and I together. After talking with my pastor about the situation, he recommended for us to begin a process of joint marriage counseling, and since our therapist refused, he said he would arrange for us to begin meeting together with one of our pastors. As a result of these events, I quit attending therapy with my first therapist after 2 years and 7 months, and my wife and I began attending counseling together with one of our pastors. Little did I know at the time how long and difficult our process of marriage counseling would turn out to be. In the end, my wife and I met together through a process that was incredibly difficult and messy, but redemptive, for an additional 3 years and 2 months.

While all this confusion, disagreement, and disillusionment was swirling around the issue of my therapy, I continued to struggle deeply with the difficult reality of physical pain in my body. I tried to live with it to the best of my ability and learn what it means to embrace pain as my friend, but at times I rebelled against my circumstances and the physical pain, and as the emotional roller coaster continued to scream through my soul, I struggled frequently with feelings and thoughts of depression, anger, and rage. I thought to myself, "Where are you, God? This is so completely unfair! What do you want from me? I'm trying so hard to do the right thing! Please help me, and please save my marriage! I just don't know how much longer I can hang in there, God." It was during one such low point in my life that I had one particular interchange with Sheri that was completely devastating to me.

We were talking about our lives and our marriage one day, as we frequently did, and I was appealing to Sheri for help on the issue of my physical pain. She knew of my vow, and she knew that I lived with almost constant pain. Although I don't remember the exact context of our discussion, or our exact words, I was trying to convey to her how difficult it was for me, and that I desperately needed her to help me with some form of physical release. She responded with words that pierced my heart like an arrow, and said something to the effect that it was my own fault, that she was not responsible for my pain, that she was completely unimpressed with my vow, and thought it was nothing more than another expression of my self-will and an attempt to manipulate her accordingly. I was crushed by the weight of her words, and in the days that followed I felt overwhelmed with hopelessness. The heavy darkness around my soul seemed to be suffocating me, and from my lonely place of depression and despair, I broke the vow I had made almost 2 years earlier. I thought to myself, "This just doesn't matter, God. I have tried to do the right thing. I have tried to honor you and to honor my wife with my body and my sexuality, and all I have received in return is pain. My wife is completely unimpressed with my vow, and apparently you are too, God, because you don't seem like you are doing anything to change our lives. Where are you, God?"

From this low point in my life, I broke the vow that had meant so much to me, and I began to masturbate again to relieve my emotional and physical pain. As I relinquished the will to continue honoring my vow, my sense of shame and despair seemed overwhelming, and I wondered if the long battle I had been fighting was all for nothing.

Chapter 30
Restitution

 One of the things we discussed and explored during my process of therapy was the principle of restitution. I had deeply hurt several people over the years through the misguided and sinful expression of my sexuality, and we discussed how I might make restitution to such people. Restitution is a biblical principle central to the Law of Moses, and is reflected numerous times throughout the Bible.

> The LORD said to Moses, "Say to the Israelites: 'When a man or woman wrongs another in any way and so is unfaithful to the LORD, that person is guilty and must confess the sin he has committed. He must make full restitution for his wrong, add one fifth to it and give it all to the person he has wronged.'" Numbers 5:5–7

> Fools mock at making amends for sin, but goodwill is found among the upright. Proverbs 14:9

> But Zacchaeus stood up and said to the Lord, "Look, Lord! Here and now I give half of my possessions to the poor, and if I have cheated anybody out of anything, I will pay back four times the amount." Luke 19:8

Although I do not claim to understand it completely, I see the principle of restitution as a reflection of the coming day of God's ultimate justice in the affairs of men — a day when every valley will be raised up, every mountain and hill made low, every crooked place made straight, and every inequity brought into the light of truth to be made right. There is something in the heart of every person that longs for such a day of reckoning, and hungers for relief from the unfairness, injustice, and abuse he or she has suffered. Something deep within the human heart seems to spontaneously cheer when the good guy wins and the bad guy is caught and required to pay for his evil deeds. I believe this intrinsic longing within the human heart for equity is completely consistent with the just character of God Himself, and reveals something of the purpose of restitution in this life. The expression of restitution allows a tangible demonstration of repentance by the offender, and a taste of heaven's future banquet of justice for the offended. As I contemplated these things and realized the truth of this principle in God's Word, I was convicted of my own need to make restitution to those whom I had offended. I knew my efforts toward compensation for losses endured at my hands would be wholly insufficient, but hoped my gestures would indicate my heartfelt regrets and in some small way repay the pain I had caused.

One of the important principles I learned regarding restitution is that the welfare of the offended party should be the highest priority, and the true goal of restitution is to serve the victim's ultimate good above my own. In other words, the purpose of restitution is not primarily so I can feel better about myself and somehow get myself off the hook for the harm I have caused, but rather it is to be a sincere act of love and humility designed to demonstrate a true heart of sorrow and repentance to the offended in the hope that such a gesture will contribute to their own healing process. Throughout my counseling process, we discussed at various times the relationships in my life where restitution could be considered, and through the thoughtful guidance of my advisers, determined what we believed to be the appropriate course of action, or non-action, in each of a variety of situations. I learned that in fact, there are certain people I've offended whom I should in no way initiate toward because such contact could cause them further pain and duress. In such circumstances, the greatest gift I can offer is my willingness to wait in silence for whenever they might initiate discussion that would then be beneficial to their healing process. For those relationships that warranted it, my making restitution with those I offended included a variety of initiatives on my behalf, including: speaking with them face-to-face in order to acknowledge the harm and pain I had caused them and to demonstrate an ownership of my sin against them; apologizing for what I had done; demonstrating a willingness to understand the pain I had caused them; writing letters to them with similar themes; offering to attend counseling sessions with them to discuss the damage done; offering to pay for their counseling sessions if they felt the need to attend counseling in order to expedite their healing process; and giving them additional funds in order to bless their lives.

As I concluded my sessions with my first therapist, one of the final acts of business we discussed was the act of restitution to one particular family I had deeply harmed by my sin. Through a series of events, this couple was attending therapy sessions with the same therapist my wife and I were seeing, and I had been aware of this fact for some period of time. I had offered for a prolonged period of time to pay for their counseling sessions, because I felt in my heart that they were in therapy, in large part, because of me. Although I had wanted to provide this gesture of repentance toward them for some period of time, the therapist had not allowed me to do so. He did not offer a detailed explanation, and simply said he thought it was not yet time for such a gesture. As the months passed and my disagreement with my therapy process escalated, and it was becoming obvious that our time together was coming to a close, my therapist brought up this issue and said he thought it was an appropriate time for me to demonstrate an act of restitution toward this particular couple. For a variety of reasons, this family had apparently been struggling financially, and the therapist thought a financial gift would greatly bless them. He suggested a particular amount of money that he thought would be an appropriate gift of restitution. I asked if I could give a greater sum, and was encouraged by my therapist and pastor to follow my heart accordingly if I was inclined to do so. I said that I wanted to talk with my wife about it first and secure her blessing on whatever amount we decided on. After doing so I wrote a check to them that was substantially greater than the amount I was counseled to give. Along with the check, I was allowed to write them a letter, and in the letter I reiterated, to the best of my ability, my heart of sorrow and repentance for the pain I had caused them. I especially wanted them to understand that in no way did I intend the gift to be a kind of payoff for my sin, but simply hoped it would be a small token of blessing to them, and demonstrate to them how sorry I was for the harm I had caused. It was a great honor for me to be able to bless them in such a fashion, and I can only hope they received and understood my gift with the same spirit of heart from which I offered it.

As an interesting side note, I was deeply blessed a couple years later as God allowed me to express my sorrow and repentance again to these beautiful people. Through a series of events, we attended the same Bible conference, and on the first night of the conference we sat near one another in the sanctuary. As the service came to a close, the worship band played, and many people sang while others were on their knees throughout the sanctuary praying with one another. It was a powerful scene and I could feel the very presence of God.

As I worshiped God, tears began streaming down my face as I struggled deeply with sadness and shame at the reality of how deeply I had hurt someone who had once been my friend. I could feel the Spirit of God telling me to go to my brother and confess to him once again, but I resisted through the first song because of the deep shadow of shame I was standing in. As the second song began, I knew the Lord wanted me to act, so I slowly moved toward my brother. As I approached him, I leaned near him and tried to whisper in his ear so he could hear me above the music. I tried to tell him I was so sorry for what I had done and for how I had hurt him, but I was unable to say the words because of my overwhelming tears. As I stood there and cried, he offered me one of the greatest and most tangible expressions of forgiveness I have ever received in my life: he put his strong arms around me in a loving embrace. I collapsed in his arms, and as I sobbed and cried he comforted me with kind words of love that I treasure to this day and that will remain confidential between the two of us. It was a precious and redemptive moment in my life, and a wonderful taste of the banquet of forgiveness that surely waits for me in heaven.

Chapter 31
Therapy II & a Crown of Thorns

 As Sheri and I began meeting with our pastor for marriage counseling, it seemed like we had diametrically opposing viewpoints on the direction we were moving, and she strongly disagreed with my decision to quit meeting with my first counselor. She felt our therapist was more qualified to counsel us than our pastor, and thought I should continue meeting with him. I felt very fervently that we needed to be in counseling together, dealing head-on with the issues in our marriage. Since that was the direction I wanted to move as her husband, and our pastors agreed it would be good for us to be in counseling together, Sheri reluctantly submitted to the guidance of her spiritual authorities and we began meeting weekly for marriage counseling, although she also continued meeting with the first therapist on her own.

As we began to meet, and the weeks passed, we talked about many different issues central to our relationship, and discussed in detail the different ways that we were hurt and disappointed in one another. At times this process was profoundly difficult and painful. It was difficult to hear my wife's heart and to face the reality of how deeply I had failed her in so many ways. It was challenging to be objective about my own sin, to see it for what it really was, and to not resort to justification, rationalization, or minimization in the attempt to candy-coat my sin and make myself not look so bad. It was difficult for me to learn the delicate balance between being a man of strength and a man of tenderness all at the same time, to confront the sin I saw in my wife's heart and life without making her feel like I was attacking her, all the while demonstrating to her that my heart was for her, and not against her. It was difficult to look at the ugliness of the sin and selfishness that lived in my heart at different times, and to see and deal with the issues that served to push my wife away from me and make her afraid of me rather than draw her toward me and allow her to trust me. During these arduous days we talked about things like the difficulty Sheri had trusting me because of my tendency to be coercive and manipulative in our relationship, her tendency to be afraid of me and to not feel safe with me because of my resentment and anger that our relationship was not how I thought it should be, her complaints about my deficiencies as both a husband and a father, my failures as the spiritual leader of our home, and my tendencies to avoid the real issues of my life through the wrongful use of various compulsions and addictions like busyness, entertainment, food, and workaholism. It was very difficult to face my wife's honest heart and words during these counseling sessions, and many times I felt enraged by the things she said about me, but I knew in my heart she knew me better than any other person on planet Earth, and God was using her like a mirror to reflect back to me my true image. I wanted more than anything else for our marriage to be healed, and through this difficult process God continued to humble me deeply as I saw and understood how seriously I had failed my wife in so many ways.

Of course, the process we were involved with was a two-way street, and I also had the opportunity to express my hurts and disappointments, and the ways I felt Sheri had deeply failed me. Near the top of my list was the issue of sex, and I continued to express how exceedingly difficult it was for me to live without sex in my life, and how deeply hurt I felt as a man by Sheri's rejection of me. As we began to talk about this issue, and our pastor began to bring some pressure to bear on Sheri for the way she had been conducting herself in this area of our lives, she became outraged and offended by his suggestions, and she came to the place where she refused to participate any longer in our counseling process. As a result, she quit attending our sessions in protest, and left me with the choice to continue meeting alone with our pastor.

At first, I was completely flabbergasted by Sheri's decision and conduct. It seemed as if our situation was more hopeless than it had ever been, and I couldn't believe Sheri would drop out because our pastor suggested that she should be willing to have sex with me. As I counseled with my pastor given this new turn of events, he challenged me to push ahead, and suggested the two of us continue meeting and focus on how God wanted to continue changing my heart and life. He said there were plenty of issues for me to work on apart from Sheri, and said that if Sheri did not want to participate, that I could still continue to do business with God and work on being the kind of man He wanted me to be. As a result, I continued to meet with my pastor for 6 months before Sheri returned to our sessions. As God's providence would have it, these 6 months became a crucial period of His working in my heart, and the Lord found an unexpected way to cut my heart even deeper during His divine surgery on me.

As we began this 6-month period, I made the decision, with my pastor's blessing and approval, to quit sleeping with my wife and to move out of our bedroom. Although I had made this move many different times throughout our difficult marriage, it was normally couched in such ugly motives as anger, punishment, self-protection, and revenge. Although the outward action was the same this time around — moving out of the bedroom — the energy of my heart was completely different. My pastor and I talked at length regarding the stature of my heart, and with this accountability I conveyed to Sheri that I was leaving our bedroom not because I wanted to, but because it was simply too difficult for me to sleep with her given our current circumstances. I told her I loved her and I thought she was beautiful. I told her I was attracted to her and that I wanted to hold her and occasionally make love to her. I told her it was simply too difficult for me to be in such a close and intimate setting without being allowed to touch her or enjoy her in any way. I tried to convey to her that I was simply too weak to handle such circumstances. I told her I longed for the day we could sleep together again, and that I wasn't sleeping in the basement to hurt or punish her, but I simply thought it was the most reasonable alternative given our current situation.

I therefore moved into the basement for an undetermined period of time, and as I did, God began to deal with my heart in a deeper way. As I continued to meet with my pastor weekly, and as I read my Bible and a couple different books God had brought to my hands, I began to discern the voice of God whispering to me, and could sense what He was asking me to do. I felt that He was inviting me to take His hand, and to walk closer to Him than I ever had before. I felt that He was inviting me to allow Him to be my all in all, and to be my complete sufficiency. I felt the Lord was inviting me to let Him be my portion, meaning I should let Him be everything to me. It's as though He was asking me, "Tony, am I enough for you? Can you still and quiet your soul before me, even if you never sleep with your wife or have sex with her again for the rest of your life? Am I enough for you? Or do you have to have me, and these other things, in order to be happy? Can you learn to be content with just our relationship? Will you seek me, and draw near to me, and let me be everything to you? Will you let me be for you what your wife is not? Will you let me fill the empty and lonely place in your heart? Can you learn to be satisfied with me?" As God drew my heart toward Himself, and as I tried to learn to let Him be everything to me, I found several verses that ministered deeply to my heart, including the following.

> Yet this I call to mind and therefore I have hope: Because of the LORD'S great love we are not consumed, for his compassions never fail. They are new every morning; great is your faithfulness. I say to myself, "The LORD is my portion; therefore I will wait for him." Lamentations 3:21–24

I wanted to let God be my portion, and I wanted to focus on being satisfied with His presence in my life rather than being dissatisfied because of the things I wanted but was unable to have. I sought the Lord every single day, and as I did I tried to focus on the beam that lived in my own eye, rather than focusing on the speck in Sheri's eye, as I had done for so many years. Each night as I walked down the basement steps to sleep alone in our guest bedroom, I struggled with the pain that lived constantly in my heart and frequently in my body, and at times I poured out my complaint to the Lord.

> Then Job replied: "Even today my complaint is bitter; his hand is heavy in spite of my groaning. If only I knew where to find him; if only I could go to his dwelling! I would state my case before him and fill my mouth with arguments. I would find out what he would answer me, and consider what he would say. Would he oppose me with great power? No, he would not press charges against me. There an upright man could present his case before him, and I would be delivered forever from my judge." Job 23:1–7

It was during one such night of wrestling with God that He found an unexpected way to pierce my heart. As I was in bed, reading my Bible and struggling with the lessons He was requiring of me, I looked up and across the room I saw a picture of Jesus I had seen many times before. Only this time it was different, because I saw it with the eyes of my heart instead of just my physical eyes. I can't explain it or prove it, but I know in my heart the Holy Spirit anointed that picture for my eyes to see, and the image pierced my heart like an arrow shot from His holy bow. "He drew his bow and made me the target for his arrows. He pierced my heart with arrows from his quiver" (Lamentations 3:12–13).

The picture was a simple black and white drawing of the head of Jesus, with His head and neck bowed, eyes closed, and a crown of thorns upon His head. Although He is in a place of pain and loneliness, there is a look of peace and surrender upon Him, and His mouth is closed in silence. Although the picture does not reveal His surroundings, I can only imagine it is minutes before His crucifixion, as the Roman soldiers mocked Him, hit Him, and spit upon Him. There is not a trace of contempt or anger upon His face. He is not poised to defend Himself, or compelled to prove His innocence, or ready to explain why everything that's happening to Him is so unfair. He is the picture of humility, brokenness, and surrender.

As my eyes soaked in the image before me, the Holy Spirit seemed to burn it into my heart, and I knew in a moment what He was saying to me. He was showing me in the image of the picture the man who I was not, and He was showing me the man He was calling me to be. "Tony, will you bow your heart and your neck and your head before me? Will you lay aside your endless words and reasonings? Will you still yourself and allow me to place a crown of thorns upon you? Will you empty yourself of contempt, anger, and self-vindication? Will you be like Jesus?" As His divine arrow pierced the center of my heart, something broke within me, and tears streamed down my face as I bowed my head before Him, and every night from then on, in a mystery, the Lord wooed my heart through His image in that picture.

CHAPTER 32

A HEART of FLESH & AN EYE of SUSPICION

The progress of God's work in my heart was significant during the 6-month period when I slept in the basement alone, as God gradually continued to help me see my sin and slowly continued changing my heart of stone to a heart of flesh. "I will give them an undivided heart and put a new spirit in them; I will remove from them their heart of stone and give them a heart of flesh" (Ezekiel 11:19).

Over the years, I often thought of my relationship with God as a kind of war within my soul. Like the Allied troops that invaded Normandy on D-Day, God had landed on the beaches of my heart through my salvation, but there were many strong resident enemies that He would be forced to fight as He attempted to win more and more of my heart to Himself. As I did battle with God through the process of sanctification over the years, there were many minor skirmishes that ended quickly as I raised the white flag of surrender to the powerful but good enemy who was conquering more of me. In such conflicts the Lord was able to gain significant portions of ground quickly as He occupied territory in my heart that was once alien to His presence and control. But, unfortunately, there were also many bloody battles that raged on violently for prolonged periods of time as I resisted surrender to what He was requiring of me. In such conflicts He would slowly push ahead,

161

capturing more of my heart inch by bloody inch. It was during the months I slept alone in the basement, confronted repeatedly by the gentle and surrendered image of Jesus in the picture, that God's work in my heart seemed to gain significant momentum as He continued to build upon the underpinnings of His efforts against me. A gifted sculptor can visualize an image of beauty within a block of marble, and though he strikes the unyielding and cold slab hundreds of times with no apparent progress, the moment eventually comes when one well-placed blow from his hammer splits his reluctant subject perfectly in two, thus forwarding his effort toward the hidden prize he is seeking. Anyone watching such a master at work would know that the single marble-splitting blow was precipitated by hundreds of previous blows. In much the same way, God's apparent lack of progress as He worked to uncover my good heart was suddenly vindicated as my heart yielded further than ever before to His persistence.

In the weeks and months that followed, I was able to conduct myself completely differently than I had for years toward Sheri. We were still not sleeping together, and we were still not making love, but somehow I had come to the place where I could say, like the words to the old hymn, "It is well with my soul." Although I broke my vow months earlier, and I masturbated occasionally in order to relieve physical pain, it seemed as though my need for sex, and my compulsive behavior regarding masturbation, was broken. I didn't struggle with lust in my heart toward other women like I had for so long, and I didn't struggle with thoughts I knew were dishonoring to God. I knew in my heart there were many issues and problems in my life that had contributed to my horrible marriage, and I saw myself more and more to blame for our current circumstances, rather than just blaming Sheri as I had done for so many years.

As I focused more on my own heart, continued my counseling sessions, and as the image of Jesus in the picture continued to do its mysterious work in my heart, something within me began to change. It seemed as if the anger that had always lived within me somehow melted away, and I was able to move toward Sheri with a different kind of heart. I saw her each day, and I talked to her with no contempt in my heart or voice. I enjoyed spending time with her, and I tried to bless her by showing her concern, helping her around the house, and by praying with her. I did not pressure her for sex, and I wasn't struggling with resenting her because of our lack of physical intimacy. I was slowly learning to still and quiet my soul before Him, to let the Lord be my portion, and He was helping me to be a better man.

A Heart of Flesh & an Eye of Suspicion   163

During the progress of these days, Sheri noticed the difference in me, but she watched me with an eye of suspicion, and rightly so. Over the years, she learned that my emotional life resembled the path of a roller coaster, and whenever I was doing well and treating her nicely, she knew it would only be a matter of time before I would cycle back through the stages of emotional revolt and resort to the predictable patterns of behavior she was so accustomed to.

Perhaps worst of all was my frequent use of words as a weapon to punish, abuse, and confuse her. When I was feeling upset or overwhelmed, it was common for me to use what came naturally to me—my ability to choose words and communicate my feelings—and to do it in a way that was verbally abusive and demeaning. I would ask Sheri a question about what was bothering her, but in reality I didn't really want to know her thoughts and feelings regarding my question. I already had a hidden agenda, and after allowing her to speak briefly, I would proceed to dump the mother lode of my powerful words and emotions all over her. At such times my energy was like a snowball rolling down a hill, getting bigger and bigger, gaining more and more momentum, and then smashing and crushing anything in its path. I could easily work myself into a kind of frenzy as I confronted Sheri with my unending questions, reasonings, explanations, and illustrations. All of this was designed to give me an upper hand as I attempted to prove that Sheri's thoughts and how she was treating me were so wrong, and how I was so right.

Although there may have been truth to some of my viewpoints and some of the things I said, I know now that how I presented myself, and the state of my heart during such frequent episodes were desperately wrong. How could Sheri possibly process what I was trying to convey when I resembled more of a monster than a man? Any value to the message I preached was completely overshadowed and disqualified because of the kind of messenger I was, and Sheri would later come to refer to her posture toward me during these frequent attacks as "circling the wagons." She apparently felt like I was an Indian, and all she could do to survive my attack was "circle the wagons" and wait for the assault of my words, like poisonous and sharp arrows, to subside. I learned in time that my frequent use of words to attack and overwhelm Sheri was one of the greatest ways that I harmed our relationship, and one of the greatest ways I pushed her away from me and made it difficult for her to trust me. Like the Old Faithful geyser in Yellowstone National Park, I naturally and frequently blew off steam whenever the pressure built up great enough on the inside, and in so doing I deeply harmed my wife through my verbal abuse. No wonder she found it difficult to feel safe with me and to enjoy my touch. No wonder she was suspicious of this new Tony who was now being so nice to her, and no wonder she was waiting in suspicion to see how long it would be before she'd have to "circle the wagons" again.

Chapter 33

The Vow II

After I had been meeting with my pastor alone for 6 months, and continued to make progress in my heart concerning how I was relating to Sheri, we agreed to invite Sheri to sit in on one session for a kind of "checkup" on how we were doing from her point of view. She agreed to do so, and after attending that initial session, she further agreed to rejoin our marriage counseling process. In the weeks that followed we continued to discuss our marital relationship, our disappointments and hurts, and the direction we were moving in our marriage. I remember Sheri acknowledging that something in my heart seemed different, and that I was treating her better than I had in a long time. She said she couldn't deny the changes that were occurring in my life, but admitted she was still suspicious of me and struggled with letting herself trust me as I attempted to move toward her in a new way. Ambivalence swirled through Sheri, as contradictory feelings of wanting to respond to me and being afraid of me simultaneously tugged at her heart. But as we continued to meet for a period of weeks that grew into months, and she continued to watch my behavior with a careful eye, Sheri's defenses against me slowly began losing their power as the handiwork of God in my heart gently wooed her toward me.

It was about this time that, much to my surprise, Sheri initiated a discussion in one of our counseling sessions. She wanted to talk about my vow to God concerning the expression of my sexuality, and my habit of masturbation. She knew of my vow, and she knew that I had broken it after almost 2 years because I was so depressed and discouraged at the time. She expressed that this was a great concern to her, and she wanted to challenge me to reinstate my vow. She said she thought the practice of masturbation was dangerous for me to participate in, and she felt in her heart that I needed to re-establish my vow before God, ending the practice completely. My initial reaction to Sheri's suggestion was strangely dichotomous, as part of me was stunned, and almost offended, that she would dare to challenge me concerning masturbation when she was clearly withholding herself from me physically and we weren't even sleeping together. Yet, at the same time, something deep in my heart was somehow pleased that this was so important to Sheri, and that she found the courage to initiate the discussion.

As we began to discuss the topic, I expressed my heart to Sheri to the best of my ability. I told her I wanted to honor God and to honor her with the expression of my sexuality. I told her I had done so for almost 2 years, and that I was sadly disappointed in myself for breaking my vow. I told her I wanted to reinstate the vow, but I was afraid of how difficult it would be for me, and I was afraid of the horrible physical pain that would result. In the context of our discussion, we began talking about the possibility of us sleeping together again. I told her that I wanted nothing more than to sleep in the same bed with her again, but that I was afraid of the conflict it would create in my heart, because I knew it would stimulate my desire for her, which would lead to further emotional turmoil and physical pain. I told her I would be willing to move back into our bedroom, and that I would be willing to reinstate my vow before God and before her, but that I needed to know that she understood how difficult it would be for me and that she would agree to help me more regularly with some form of physical release. Sheri objected at first and complained that my request was unfair because it placed too much pressure on her, and she thought my vow should be between me and God, regardless of what she did or didn't do. I told her I agreed with her in one sense, but in another sense I disagreed. I told her that she alone had held complete power over our sexual lives and activity since our wedding night so many years ago, and that she still held supreme power over that area of our lives. I told her that just as she had trouble learning to trust me again, that it was difficult for me to trust her with so much power over my life. I told her I was afraid that if I made my vow, that she would maintain supreme control over our sexual intimacy, she would never have sex with me, and I would suffer as the result, just as I did during the first 2 years of my previous vow. I told her it was unfair for her to have so much power over me, and it was unfair that I would have to suffer. I told her that I didn't think my request of her was unfair, or that it placed too much pressure on her, because God had given her to me as my helpmate, I wasn't supposed to live my life without sex, and it wasn't up to me to face this battle alone. I appealed to her and told her that I would have a much better chance of succeeding in my vow if I knew that I wasn't facing it alone, but that I would be facing it with her by my side, knowing that she also was committed to my success.

As we discussed these things, I think we both began to see that it was unfair for either one of us to expect the other to assume the full weight of responsibility for our sex life. I saw that it was unrealistic for me to expect Sheri to give me complete access to her body anytime I wanted it, because she was still in the process of her own healing, and she was still learning to trust me with her heart and her body. Sheri began to see how unfair it was for her to expect me to reinstate my vow, and to move back into our bedroom, with no assurance from her that she was going to help me more regularly with the expression of my sexuality. As a result, Sheri came to the place where although she said that she could not guarantee it, she agreed to do her very best, by God's grace, to make love with me at least once a week. I told her that on the strength of this commitment, I would be willing to move back into our bedroom, and so I did.

CHAPTER 34

The Schedule & the Fury of Hell

It was absolutely wonderful for me to move back into the same bedroom with Sheri, and I deeply enjoyed our physical closeness after sleeping apart and living with the sense of distance that had defined our relationship for so long. When I say I enjoyed the physical closeness between the two of us, I'm not just referring to being close to her in bed. I'm referring to the great pleasure I received from just being near Sheri wherever we were — snuggling up close to her at night, smelling her hair, holding hands with her while driving, taking occasional walks with her, and sitting next to her at social events. As we continued to work on our marriage, and as we slowly moved toward one another in a new way emotionally and relationally, we were also learning how to move toward one another and enjoy one another physically, and as Sheri had committed, we began to make love once a week. This went on for some period of time, and as we continued to go to counseling, I soon lobbied to increase our lovemaking to twice a week. Since I had re-established my vow, my sexual expression was limited only to Sheri, and I quickly learned that my body's natural rhythm ran on a three- to four-day cycle. If I had to wait longer than that, I usually encountered pretty serious discomfort and pain. As a result, I was typically required to live in pain for several days while I anxiously waited for the new week to officially roll around. Making matters worse, when it was finally time for us to make love again, the event was overshadowed by my physical pain, which made it difficult for me to relax and enjoy the

169

process and resulted in the event concluding much sooner than I desired. I reasoned that making love twice per week would eliminate these other challenges since there would then be a physical release every three to four days. I promised Sheri that if we could increase to twice per week, I would be satisfied for a prolonged period of time, and I would not ask or pressure her in any way for three times a week. Sheri rather reluctantly agreed to try, and so we set up a schedule, and began to make love twice per week.

As things worked out, we ended up being on this schedule for just over a year and a half. Although a schedule to make love was far less than ideal, it seemed appropriate for us at the time because of our difficult history. Sheri was still growing in her personal healing, and she was still learning to trust and feel comfortable with me as her husband. Although she had come a long way in her healing process, she still seemed incapable at the time of responding to me naturally and spontaneously, and the schedule provided a sense of security for her that allowed her to know what to expect and when.

Although I personally wasn't crazy about our love life being determined by an agreed upon schedule, I felt it was still one thousand percent better under such circumstances than it had been for the first 15 or so years of our marriage. After living without sex for such prolonged periods of time, for so many long years, I was completely delighted to have a steady diet of sexual expression on a weekly basis. This was like heaven to me compared to our past, and I therefore readily agreed to the schedule. In addition, I knew that God had worked deeply in my heart through the dark valley I had been walking the past several years. I knew that God had broken the chains of sexual bondage that had held me captive since my childhood, and He was helping me to be a new and better man. I was upholding my vow before God and my wife, and I took great satisfaction in knowing that I was honoring both through my sexuality. If there was any sexual expression in my life, it was with my wife only. I believed that's the place that God had brought me, and that's what God was requiring of me. As I lived out the expression of how God had worked in my heart and changed me, I was satisfied to know that God was receiving honor from the very area of my life from which I had dishonored Him for so many years.

We continued on this schedule for just over a year and a half, and it was then that we hit a major bump in the road, as the fury of hell itself seemed to come against us. We were doing so well that we had decided sometime previous, with our pastor's approval, to discontinue counseling. At the time, we had been in counseling with him for just over 3 years, and at that point we had been consistently making love according to our schedule for over a year. We were doing so much better, in many ways, than ever, and we felt it was appropriate for us to jettison into the reality and adventure of life on our own after almost 6 years of continuous therapy. Our pastor released us from counseling with his blessing, and we mutually agreed to visit with him and have a kind of "checkup" every several months thereafter, as necessary.

After being out of counseling for about 6 months, and keeping our schedule accordingly, Sheri suddenly froze up in her ability to respond to me, and she was unable to continue with our schedule. When we tried to talk about it, she was unable to express in words the turmoil alive in her soul and she only said that she couldn't keep our schedule any longer, and that she did not know when or if we would be able to make love again.

As the reality and implications of Sheri's words seemed to hit me head-on, like a powerful steam roller smashing full force into me, I responded in a terrible way that I am rather ashamed to admit. I was almost immediately gripped with intense panic as I felt the progress we had fought for so hard to achieve over the past several years was suddenly slipping away. My panic so quickly tightened its grip on me and almost choked the life out of me when I realized to my horror there was nothing I could do to stop what was happening. I tried to talk to Sheri and understand what was happening, but she was unable to communicate clearly with me at the time because she herself didn't understand what was going on inside of her. I knew in my heart my attempt to corral the situation was completely useless, and as I desperately grasped for answers and understanding from Sheri, it felt as though I was trying to catch and hold in my hand the smoke from a burning campfire.

The panic that had visited itself upon me brought some dark companions along, and in the days that followed I felt swallowed up, as a familiar shroud of darkness, despair, and hopelessness settled upon me. Like a prisoner in a concentration camp whom the enemy is trying to break through the use of propaganda, an endless stream of voices blared at me over the loudspeaker of my mind in the days that followed. "Your marriage isn't fixed. You have not made any progress. You are all the way back to square one. Everything you have been through over the past several years has been in vain. Sheri is not healed. Sheri has not changed. She will never be able to make love with you again. She will always be in bondage. God has not saved you, and God has not saved your marriage. God has failed you. God does not care about you. God is nowhere to be found, and He is powerless. You are going to have to start completely over again. It will be years and years of more struggle and pain for you. You will never be happy with this woman. Do you remember the physical pain you endured? You will be faced with more pain, and you will never be able to escape it. Everything is useless. You have come this far, for what? For nothing! You have tried so hard, for what? For nothing! You might as well forget about ever having a happy marriage. There is no way you can face the future. You better give up. You better get as far away from this marriage as you can, as fast as you can. You might as well get divorced and get it over with, because things will never get better. Sheri doesn't want you. She doesn't care about you. She doesn't care about your needs or your pain. This marriage is a disaster, and it will never get better. Your life is a miserable wreck and a failure. You would be better off if you were dead."

As the weight of the legions of overpowering thoughts and voices crushed upon me day after day, I despaired of life itself, and I remember one exceptionally devastating exchange with Sheri. We were sitting in our bedroom talking one morning, and as the dark and hopeless despair that swirled around my soul tightened its ugly grip, I literally found it difficult to breathe, and with tears streaming down my face and an indescribable weight of emotional pain in my chest, I began to sob through my tears that I didn't want to live anymore. It seemed as though the deepest place of my heart had broken open, and as it did, the emotions and words sobbed out of my mouth. "I don't want to live anymore. I want to die. If this is my life, I do not want it anymore. Please God, let me die. I can't do this anymore. If we are going back to the beginning, and have to start all over again, I cannot do it. I don't want this pain anymore. I want to die. Please God, let me die." I had never so sincerely and passionately longed for death, and Sheri began to cry as she realized how serious my words were.

It's as though all the difficulty of my past — the sin, pain, abuse, disappointment, hurt, disillusionment, anger, fear, suffering, and heartache — was all mysteriously piled up in a giant mountain, and somehow I was being asked to turn around and face the mountain and to begin climbing all over again. The prospect of such a monumental journey was simply overwhelming to me, and I knew in my heart I would rather be dead than be required to face such an impossible mountain again. I felt utterly disappointed because I thought we had come so far. I knew that we had faced the mountain of pain and had climbed for so long, and I thought we had made progress, crossed the summit, and that we were on the downward descent. We had been doing so much better in our relationship, and we had been

THE SCHEDULE & THE FURY OF HELL   **173**

making love consistently every week for the past year and a half, and suddenly all our progress seemed to vanish overnight. When Sheri rebelled
against our established schedule, and said she couldn't have sex with me anymore, it felt as though the whole world was crashing in upon me. It was from
this place of dark and hopeless despair that death tried to take me by the
hand, and as I looked in his dark and sunken eyes, I didn't even feel afraid.
"The cords of death entangled me; the torrents of destruction overwhelmed
me. The cords of the grave coiled around me; the snares of death confronted me" (Psalm 18:4–5).

There was a time in my life when I couldn't understand or relate to people who wanted to die, or to people who committed suicide. I saw them as
weak and confused people who were too feeble to manage life and make the
best of things. I saw them as failures, and looked at them through eyes of
contempt and superiority, but not anymore. I now understand, because of
my own life experience, how a person can become so completely overwhelmed with life and the endless pain this world has to offer, that he begins
to see death as a viable option. I cannot judge such people anymore. I can
only feel a heart of compassion for them, and hope they find a sense of relief
from their torturous pain. I can also understand, because of my own experience, why so many great people in the Bible struggled with thoughts and
desires for death, including Jonah (Jonah 4:3,8), David (Psalm 116:3–4),
Job (Job 3), Jeremiah (Jeremiah 20:14–18), Moses (Numbers 11:10–15),
and the Apostle Paul (II Corinthians 1:8).

Of course, I am in no way advocating death as a reasonable or viable
alternative to life's pain. I'm only saying that I can understand why people
are tempted to escape the pain of life through the doorway of death. I believe
there is a very real enemy against us, and his primary objective in these days
is to hurt the heart of God by attacking, destroying, and killing those whom
God loves the most, namely you and me. Through the progress of these dark
days, I knew there was a very real battle waging over my soul. I knew the
devil was once again lying to me, attempting to destroy my life, and trying
to discredit the handiwork that God was accomplishing in our lives and marriage. Rather than believing his lies, I chose instead to hold on tight and to
cry out to the One who had already rescued me so many times before.

> The cords of death entangled me; the torrents of destruction
> overwhelmed me. The cords of the grave coiled around me;
> the snares of death confronted me. In my distress I called to

the LORD; I cried to my God for help. From his temple he heard my voice; my cry came before him, into his ears... He reached down from on high and took hold of me; he drew me out of deep waters. He rescued me from my powerful enemy, from my foes, who were too strong for me. They confronted me in the day of my disaster, but the LORD was my support. He brought me out into a spacious place; he rescued me because he delighted in me. Psalm 18:4–6, 16–19

Chapter 35
The Power of Prayer

After doing so much better for so long, it seemed as if our forward progress was suddenly lost at Sheri's insurgence against our schedule. Since Sheri struggled with understanding what was happening in her own heart, and I was basically gripped with panic and despair by such turn of events, I didn't know what to do but call my pastor and seek his advice. We agreed to meet, and the next week Sheri and I met with two of our pastors together. As we discussed the recent circumstances of our relationship, two issues surfaced that contributed to Sheri's difficulty in responding to me.

The first issue was Sheri's complaint that I had been exceptionally frustrated, angry, and irritable for some period of time. She said it was becoming increasingly difficult for her and the boys to be around me, and it made it hard for her to want to be close to me or for her to enjoy my touch. Although Sheri had been trying to convey this to me for some period of time, I tended to disagree with her assessment of how difficult I had been to live with, and I minimized her complaint several times by basically ignoring it. She went on to convey that it was hard for her to tiptoe around me in fear during the day, and then be able to jump in bed with me and feel comfortable giving herself to me at night. As we discussed these things, I was convicted by Sheri's words, and finally realized that there was truth to what she had been saying all along. Although the details don't justify my behavior, my life had been under an unusual amount of stress for several reasons, and that stress was apparently contributing to the level of frustration I was feeling and displaying at home.

One was that my relationship with my father was worse at the time than it had ever been in my life. Without sharing all the gory details, suffice it to say that my father was extremely angry at me because we suffered a serious disagreement, and as a result he broke off his relationship with me. He saw my refusal to agree with him as a betrayal, and I saw it as establishing proper boundaries that were way overdue in our very difficult relationship.

In the end, my relationship with my father remained broken for a period of almost 2 years, and in fact remained broken until the day of his death, which occurred while writing this book. During the course of this 2-year period, the situation with my father weighed very heavily upon me, and I struggled deeply with wanting our relationship to be restored but feeling powerless in my ability to change reality. The situation required significant emotional energy for me to deal with, and no doubt contributed to my level of frustration and my short fuse at home.

An additional stressor for me at the time was the fact that we were having our dream home built. As the project progressed, it took on a life of its own. Our budget continued to expand, along with the options to be included in the house, and it soon became a project that demanded continuous time and considerable attention.

The other issue that surfaced through our discussion with our pastors was a sense of pressure Sheri was feeling in concert with our much-anticipated new home. The house was to have a large masterbedroom with a see-through fireplace into a glorious masterbathroom. The bathroom was to include an elevated and heart-shaped whirlpool tub, surrounded by marble and beautiful Roman columns. It would be an exceptional masterbedroom suite, and Sheri was beginning to feel a sense of pressure because we would soon be moving into such a luxurious and romantic bedroom. It made her feel like I would raise my expectations of our love life. It's as if her heart was slowly posturing itself into a position of self protection as she feared I would require of her endless romantic evenings filled with bubble baths, warm fires, and never-ending passion. As she adopted this image in her mind, in part because of the occasional comments I made regarding my anticipation of our new bedroom, a growing sense of pressure weighed on her because she knew in her heart she wasn't ready to be the woman she pictured in the image and feared she could never live up to such a new level of performance.

As a result of these two factors — my angry irritability and the sense of pressure Sheri had been feeling — she began to slowly shut down emotionally and physically and seemed increasingly incapable of responding to me, which led to her ultimate revolt against our scheduled lovemaking. As we discussed these various issues, it became clear that I had further business I needed to do with both God and my wife, so I apologized to her and promised I would work hard in the days ahead on controlling my anger and irritability. I also assured her that although we were moving into our new and beautiful home, and I was hopeful that our love life could continue to blossom and become more and more of what we both longed for, that I would not project upon her some new level of sexual expectation that she would be incapable of providing.

While our pastors were concerned about my behavior, and challenged me to continue working on the areas of my life that had been bothering Sheri, they were also concerned about Sheri's willingness to withdraw from me physically as a result, and after further discussion, it was decided our pastors would pray over each one of us separately. I thought this was a wonderful idea for a couple different reasons.

First, I remained convinced of the importance of submission to spiritual authority in our lives, and I felt that having our pastors lay hands on us and pray over us would be significant in assuring that we were remaining directly under the mysterious protection provided by submission to our God-given authorities. I hoped that the posture of our physical bodies during such a prayer meeting — one of humility with bended knees, bowed necks, and hanging heads — would be representative of the posture of our hearts before God, our pastors, and one another, and would ensure God's continued blessing and guidance in our lives.

Secondly, although I had always struggled with maintaining a consistent and passionate prayer life throughout my Christian experience, I nevertheless believed — and still do believe — deeply in the power of prayer. Throughout the course of my Christian life, I was involved in two different situations that involved the direct and obvious manifestation of demonic spirits, and in both situations it was absolutely amazing to see and hear the response of the demons when the Christians involved began to pray. In both situations the demons that had manifested themselves literally began to shriek, scream, and basically totally freak out in the presence of prayer. Firsthand involvement in these situations had pushed my faith in the power of prayer from my head directly into my heart, and I have remained convinced to this very day that most Christians tend to underestimate the significance

178   STORIES: THE REDEMPTION OF ONE MAN'S WOUNDED SEXUALITY

and power at our disposal through the weapon of prayer. For these reasons, I knew in my heart that if our pastors prayed over us it would be a compelling and significant step for us. Of course, over the years we had prayed many prayers for our marriage, and many people had also prayed on our behalf, but it seemed as if God was leading us at this time into a special season of prayer.

Since Sheri is a woman, and could understandably feel some sense of insecurity about having men pray over her regarding such personal and intimate issues as her sexuality, she was encouraged to invite a couple of her closest friends to her prayer meeting, which she did. Sheri's prayer meeting was held 2 weeks later, and a week later my prayer meeting occurred. In the interim, Sheri went to Dallas, Texas with our boys to visit my brother and his family. While in Dallas, Sheri participated in a prayer meeting with several godly women who are real prayer warriors and actually have a ministry of prayer and teaching others to pray. These women met with Sheri specifically to pray over her and our marriage. Although I am not privy to the exact details of that meeting, it was apparently a very powerful experience, and Sheri viewed it with such significance that she asked me one month later if she could return to Dallas specifically to meet with these women and have them pray over her again. Of course, I encouraged Sheri to go. That meant that all together, four different significant prayer meetings happened in our lives over one month. Without really trying to schedule these prayer meetings, they seemed to rather spontaneously occur. I believe in retrospect that these prayer meetings were a significant stepping-stone for God's continued work in our lives. They represented God's provision as He nurtured us through the difficult time and spiritual attack we had been under.

Another significant event that occurred revolved around a special book that God brought into my life. The book was *The Power of a Praying Husband* by Stormie Omartian. When Sheri returned to Dallas for her second prayer meeting, my brother sent a copy of this book back for me. It's a book that teaches men how to stand in their God-given position of spiritual authority in their marriage, and specifically how to pray with and over their wives. He said that he had been using this book to help him pray over his wife, and it gave him an effective and tangible expression of his love for his wife and seemed to be drawing them closer. When I got the book, I immediately began to read it, and felt compelled to begin praying over my wife every day like never before.

In the book, Omartian lists 20 different areas of your wife's life that you can begin praying over. It provides commentary and teaching on each area, as well as a list of verses related to that particular topic, along with an actual published prayer to pray over your wife. As I began to use the book, and began to pray over my wife daily for a period of weeks, I realized it was helping me progress in my God-given position of authority in my wife's life, in much the same way the "tracks" might help a train know which way it is supposed to go. A locomotive is very powerful and capable of accomplishing a tremendous amount of work, but it would be completely useless if it had no tracks and all it did was waste all of its potential by pointlessly sitting. I knew in my heart that for far too long I had wasted my God-given power and authority in my wife's life, and Omartian's book helped me to find and assume my proper role, as it provided direction for me as I began standing in a place of power, protection, and covering over my wife.

Sheri revealed to me months later that it was a very meaningful experience for her when I began consistently praying over her, and she sensed and believed that my prayers were more powerful and freeing in her life than the totality of all the other prayer meetings. She said she had an image in her mind that she was walking down a path through a very scary place surrounded by darkness, demons, and danger, but when I was praying over her she saw me as a great warrior carrying a mighty shield and sword in front of her, and she described that she felt a tremendous sense of protection, security, and safety as a result.

I believe the cumulative effect and timing of all the prayers that were offered through these various prayer meetings, along with the guidance I discovered through Omartian's book, were somehow mysteriously significant in God's unfolding plan of redemption for our lives. We had already made significant progress over the past several years as God had worked deeply in both of our hearts and our marriage. Based upon the foundation of the progress God had already achieved in each one of our hearts, it's as though He had brought us to the place where it was time for some deeper work to be accomplished in each of us through the mystery of prayer. Although we had come a long, long way, it's as though we needed this season of prayer in our lives for God to further weaken the invisible chains of bondage that still attempted to hold us in places of captivity. Although I do not know the exact details of what happened in Sheri's prayer meetings, I know what happened in mine, and I believe our adversary's strength was seriously damaged as the power of prayer was systematically unleashed against the various areas of our lives that were prayed over. In these various meetings, and with the direction of Omartian's book, we prayed for the following: a spirit of repentance, a spirit of forgiveness, the breaking of bondages and curses, victory over the power of generational sin, release and freedom from sexual bondages, defeat of controlling and manipulative spirits and tendencies, replacement of hearts of stone with hearts of flesh, a spirit of discernment and spiritual protection, God's blessing and healing, and our future.

I'm sure I won't understand the true value of all these prayers until I get to heaven. With the limited vision I am confined to in this life, however, I already know and believe they were of supreme significance. These prayers allowed me to sense a "cleanness" from the water of prayer that had washed over and through my soul, my wife, and my marriage. In the following days, it became clear that the enemy's attempt to attack us and our "schedule" was a very bad tactical move on his behalf. It's as though he didn't like the progress we were making through our schedule, so he attacked us with a fury. But in the end, God was able to take that very attack and our apparent setback, and through the resulting season of prayer, prepare us for the place of blessing he was moving us toward.

CHAPTER 36

Joel 2 & a New Beginning

When Sheri and I reached the season of prayer reflected upon in the previous chapter, we had been married for 17 years. I had made my initial confession about 6 years prior, which was the eleventh year of our marriage, and it seemed at times that the long and dark valley we had been traveling through since our wedding day would never end. At about the time of my confession, as we were just beginning our counseling process, God gave Sheri and I a promise for our marriage. The promise is found in Joel Chapter 2, and we believed at the time, despite the apparently insurmountable and difficult circumstances that surrounded us, that God was promising us He was going to save and redeem our marriage. As things worked out, and our healing process ever so slowly unfolded over the difficult years that followed, there were many days that seemed so dark and hopeless that the promise God gave us seemed to be a powerless counterfeit. Nevertheless, we continued to persevere even though there were so many times we both wanted to give up. As we slowly moved forward in our healing process, we sensed there was light at the end of our dark valley, and it seemed as if the promise God gave us so many years ago might really come to pass.

Joel was an Old Testament prophet whose mission was to call the unfaithful nation of Judah back to a place of repentance and blessing in her relationship with God. As the book opens, Chapter 1 depicts God's judgment upon the people because of their adultery and rebellion against the

181

Lord. The people had moved far from God in their hearts as they pursued a host of lesser gods and counterfeit lovers. God, in His jealousy, attempted to get His people's attention and draw their hearts back to Himself through a strange gift found in a plague of locusts. Judah was an agricultural society dependent on grape, olive, and wheat crops for its livelihood. Thus, God carried out His judgment on Judah by bringing a great army of locusts against the fields.

> The fields are ruined, the ground is dried up; the grain is destroyed, the new wine is dried up, the oil fails. Despair, you farmers, wail, you vine growers; grieve for the wheat and the barley, because the harvest of the field is destroyed. The vine is dried up and the fig tree is withered; the pomegranate, the palm, and the apple tree — all the trees of the field are dried up. Surely the joy of mankind is withered away. Joel 1:10–12

At the end of Chapter 1 and the beginning of Chapter 2, Joel invites the people of Judah — from the children to the elders — to humble themselves and come back to a place of broken repentance before the Lord.

> "Even now," declares the LORD, "return to me with all your heart, with fasting and weeping and mourning." Rend your heart and not your garments. Return to the LORD your God, for he is gracious and compassionate, slow to anger and abounding in love, and he relents from sending calamity. Who knows? He may turn and have pity and leave behind a blessing — grain offerings and drink offerings for the LORD your God. Joel 2:12–14

Joel then promises that if the people would go through this process of repentance, that the Lord would bring them back to a place of blessing, healing, and wholeness. This beautiful passage culminates in the very promise that God gave Sheri and I for our marriage: if the people repent, the Lord will return to them what the locusts had stolen.

> Be glad, O people of Zion, rejoice in the LORD your God, for he has given you the autumn rains in righteousness. He sends you abundant showers, both autumn and spring rains, as before. The threshing floors will be filled with grain; the

Joel 2 & a New Beginning   183

vats will overflow with new wine and oil. I will repay you for the years the locusts have eaten — the great locust and the young locust, the other locusts and the locust swarm — my great army that I sent among you. You will have plenty to eat, until you are full, and you will praise the name of the LORD your God, who has worked wonders for you; never again will my people be shamed. Joel 2:23–26

Through the remarkable promise in Joel that He gave us so many years ago, Sheri and I understood more clearly God's handiwork in our hearts and our marriage. We came to see how our lives, like the fields in Judah, were lying in desolation because of the generational sin, curses, and bondages that held us each captive, and the sinful autonomy, rebellion, and idolatry that lived in our hearts. We had so many problems on the inside of us that reached all the way back into our childhoods — things that God, as the Master Surgeon, determined to free us from in order to make our hearts truly His own. We came to see that God had called us into a deep and profoundly difficult process of repentance — a process in which He required things of us far beyond anything we ever anticipated, and one in which He cut deeper into our hearts than we ever imagined. And, as the result, we slowly began to see how God was bringing to pass the promise He had given us so many years ago. He was beginning to send abundant showers and autumn rains of righteousness into our lives. These showers were watering the barren and hard ground of our hearts and causing the fields that had been dry and desolate for so long to sprout and turn green. These showers were causing the grape vineyards, the olive orchards, and the wheat fields to burst forth and overflow with an abundance of new wine, oil, and grain. These showers were bringing us from a place of bondage and death to a place of freedom and life. These showers were freeing our hearts to passionately love and serve the true God rather than the legion of false gods we had been blindly devoted to. These showers were bringing us from the place of desolation and ruin to the place of prosperity and blessing. The path He had led us on was a strange and difficult journey indeed, and the allies He used in His battle against us were such unexpected forces like pain, suffering, darkness, and swarms of locusts; yet, as we continued to grope forward with Him by faith, we learned and began to see that He is a God who could repay us for the years the locusts had stolen from us.

As the season of prayer God had brought us through was coming to a close, and as Sheri and I continued to move toward one another by talking and sharing our hearts with one another, we sensed it was time to abandon our schedule completely. We did so as an expression of the new beginning God seemed to be giving our marriage. We began to journey by faith into the adventure of making love together on a regular and more spontaneous basis — which was a wonderful freedom that we were unable to enjoy for the first 17 years of our marriage.

CHAPTER 37

Divine Sex & the Future

 Although Sheri and I are doing better in our marriage than ever before, I must confess that at times we still struggle in our relationship and with our love life. I wish I could end my story with tales of never-ending romance and passionate nights of endless lovemaking, then conclude with the final words, "And they lived happily ever after," but I can't. Those words belong only at the end of fairy tales, and I'm not sure how practical they are for real people living real lives. It's true that our relationship is better than ever — we spend lots of time together, we go on dates every week, we hold hands and go for walks, we talk about our future as we share our hopes and dreams with one another, we pray together more than ever, we frequently laugh together and at times cry together, we're more united as parents than ever, and we make love on a regular and more spontaneous basis. I feel more at one with Sheri than I have ever felt, and although I can't describe it, sometimes when we're apart, I have a strange feeling in my soul. It's as if part of me feels all alone because she isn't with me, yet at the same time I feel her inside me and know that she is with me, because our souls are somehow becoming one. I'm deeply grateful that God was able to take us, two people who were at one time so distant from one another, and somehow blend our hearts and souls together as one.

Although the beauty of God's handiwork in our hearts is evident to us every day, and we frequently sense God's fingerprints on our lives, we are also reminded regularly that we still live in a fallen world, that we are each married to a broken and wounded person, and that we will never find the true sanctuary of Eden in this life. At times my heart still feels the pain of rejection and the tenderness of past wounds when I sense a kind of distance between Sheri and I. At times I suspect that she is giving herself to me because of "duty" rather than "desire," and I recurrently struggle with the apparent lack of freedom and sense of rigidity that sometimes accompanies our lovemaking. At times I feel Sheri's body close to mine, but sense that her soul — the real Sheri — is somehow mysteriously absent. Although we have come so incredibly far in our healing process, I know that God wants to work deeper in both of our hearts as He continues to "bind up the broken-hearted, to proclaim freedom to the captives, and release from darkness those who have been in prison" (Isaiah 61:1). At times I fail Sheri because of my "fallenness," and at times she fails me, but through it all we remain deeply grateful for God's handiwork in our lives and have a growing sense of awe for who He is and what He has done. In the words of Steven Curtis Chapman's powerful song, *Remember Your Chains,* "There is no one more thankful to sit at the table than the one who best remembers hunger's pain, and no heart loves greater than the one that is able to recall the time when all it knew was shame...."[1] When a soldier is severely wounded in battle, the injuries may eventually heal, but the scars and a kind of limp can remain, serving as a continual reminder of his painful past. In the same way, an alcoholic must live with the continuous remembrance and awareness of the tragedy of his past, the reality of his own frailty, and the ever-present possibility of failing. In one sense he is free from his past and the bondage that once held him, but in another sense he will never be free in this life.

When I reflect upon the terrible circumstances that surrounded our marriage, the influences that aligned Sheri and I against one another sexually, and the events that set us up for an unexpected head-on collision on our very wedding night, the image of a Christmas gift comes to mind. The essence of this image is the idea that the most important thing about a Christmas gift is the gift itself that is hidden within the wrapping. The gift usually comes in a beautiful package that might include colorful paper, attractive ribbons, and lovely bows. Although the gift wrap is invariably beautiful, we nonetheless eagerly rip through the outward package in our search to find the true prize that we know is somewhere within. As I reflect on this image, it occurs to me that sex within marriage is a lot like a Christmas gift. I further understand more clearly how terribly unprepared I was for marriage and how deeply I failed Sheri through my improper attitudes and expectations regarding sex. In the beginning of our relationship, and for many years into our marriage, I was in fact more interested in the wrapping — which was Sheri's body — than I was in the true gift hidden inside — which was Sheri's heart and soul. Of course, I loved Sheri as a person, but there were many problems with the sexual energy that lived in my heart and how I moved toward Sheri as a result. It would be years into our marriage, as one of the many manifestations of God's redemptive work in my life, that I would slowly begin learning to cherish and pursue Sheri's heart more than her body, and the very act of lovemaking would become more about our souls touching and dancing than just our physical bodies becoming one. I am still slowly learning that our lovemaking is an opportunity for me to be intimately and tenderly close to my wife, to enjoy her presence and warmth, and to enjoy her as a person. I am learning to let my breath be taken away by the intrigue, mystery, and beauty of who my wife is as an image-bearer of God, and that making love is more about pursuing her as the ultimate prize rather than her body, which is made of dust and will one day fade away.

These are lessons that are profoundly difficult for me to learn because of the person I was and the wrongness that lived within me. They are lessons God is still slowly teaching me as He continues to execute His work in me like a Master Surgeon and as He continues to change me from the man I was into the man He wants me to be.

In spite of all these things, when I reflect upon where we are today compared to where we used to be, and when I reflect upon the long and dark journey God has brought us through, I stand utterly amazed at how faithful God has been to us and how deeply He has worked in my heart. In a mystery, He has somehow captured and made my heart His own, and He has redeemed the deepest and most broken places of my life. He has saved my marriage and He is restoring to us the years the locusts stole from us. He is bringing us into a spacious place of freedom and blessing, as we continue to learn what it means to experience "divine sex" that has the blessing and favor of God upon it. He has redeemed my broken sexuality, and by His grace, He is continuing to help me honor Him and my wife through the expression of my sexuality as I now approach the 3-year anniversary of my renewed vow.

In one sense, my life story reflected through this book is more about God delivering me from the bondage of sexual addiction than it is about the healing of my marriage, but in reality the two are inextricably linked. It's amazing for me to see and realize that the healing of my sexual bondage is the thing that seemed to empower God's ability to heal my marriage. As I learned to cooperate with the Master Surgeon's necessary and painful surgery within me, it allowed Him to proceed to the next step, and He then began to rescue my failing marriage. It's as if God had to fix me first, before He could fix my marriage. The final result, nevertheless, remains the same, and I stand in awe of what He has done for me — the redemption of both my broken sexuality and my troubled marriage.

---

1 Steven Curtis Chapman's album, *Heaven in the Real World,* 1994, Sparrow Records.

Chapter 38

Enemy Fire

For these commands are a lamp, this teaching is a light, and the corrections of discipline are the way to life, keeping you from the immoral woman, from the smooth tongue of the wayward wife. Do not lust in your heart after her beauty or let her captivate you with her eyes, for the prostitute reduces you to a loaf of bread, and the adulteress preys upon your very life. Can a man scoop fire into his lap without his clothes being burned? Can a man walk on hot coals without his feet being scorched? Proverbs 6:23–28

Be self-controlled and alert. Your enemy the devil prowls around like a roaring lion looking for someone to devour. Resist him, standing firm in the faith, because you know that your brothers throughout the world are undergoing the same kind of sufferings. I Peter 5:8–9

As I have continued to walk in my vow before God and my wife, and I have continued to honor them both through the expression of my sexuality, I have experienced more freedom in the sexual area of my life than I have ever known before. I'm almost afraid to say this, however, because I'm afraid something could change overnight, and I know that I must live with constant awareness of my past and the man I was and where I have come from. The Bible says, "So, if you think you are standing firm, be careful that you don't fall!" (I Corinthians 10:12), and I know the depth of depravity I am capable of achieving apart from the grace of God in my life. Nevertheless, I stand utterly amazed by what God has accomplished in my heart, my sexuality, and my marriage. I have not expressed my sexuality, including masturbation, apart from my wife for almost 5 years at this writing[1]. I walk in virtual freedom from lust toward other women, and seldom struggle with sinful thoughts or preoccupations. When I do notice something or someone that tries to pull my heart and mind into temptation, I am empowered by the Spirit to quickly catch myself, and turn my eyes, my thoughts, and my attention elsewhere. Sheri has captured my heart, and she alone is the object of my intimate thoughts, desires, and actions. I am committed to walking in the light, in complete honesty and vulnerability to my wife, and on the few occasions I have felt tempted in the slightest way toward impure thoughts or opportunities, I have immediately shared with Sheri what was happening in my heart. In such instances, with the reinforcement of her prayer and support, I have been able to continue to walk with purity of heart, mind, and action. I feel incapable of conveying the wonderful and exhilarating sense of liberty and cleanness I feel at the very center of my soul, or the sense of freedom I feel as the result of walking in the light and knowing that there is not one single thing I am hiding from God, my wife, or my friends. It feels pure. It feels holy. It feels clean. It feels right. For all these things I am deeply thankful, and I give all the praise and glory to God for the great things He has done!

The fact is that God is winning in my heart, and in view of the great victories God is accomplishing in my life, I am learning firsthand that the devil is a sore loser. As I have continued to grow in my healing process and God has continued to redeem my life, the devil has fought back in his attempt to keep the chains of sexual bondage locked around my soul, as he has settled me squarely in the sights of his enemy fire on several different occasions.

The first such attack occurred in conjunction with a piece of rental property we own. Our tenant at the time, who was living in the house when we bought it, was a biker kind of guy, with long hair, tattoos, and an apparently wild lifestyle. He was behind on his rent, and therefore, when he called me one day to indicate he had some money for me, I was anxious to get it while the getting was good. Although he normally mailed his rent check to me each month, he said I could stop by and pick it up if I wanted to, and since I was going to be in his neighborhood later that day, I told him I'd just stop by. When I did stop, I knocked on the door and I was surprised to be greeted by an attractive young woman who I had never seen before. She was wearing a very loose-fitting and low-cut blouse and obviously wasn't wearing a bra. When I told her who I was and what I was doing, she told me that her boyfriend wasn't home, that she didn't know when he would be back, and much to my surprise, as we continued to chat for several moments, she suddenly bent over toward me in a blatantly unsubtle attempt to let me see whatever I wanted to see. My eyes had a grandstand view of the show, and I was momentarily stunned by what had suddenly occurred. I quickly realized the scene was totally uncool, pointed my eyes in another direction, stammered that I would check back later with her boyfriend, and quickly retreated to the safety of my car. Of course, I didn't know for sure what her exact intentions were, or if she would have allowed anything further to happen between the two of us had I chosen to react differently to her actions, but I really didn't care to know or understand her intentions. I knew I had to escape the situation as quickly as possible, and as I drove away, I immediately called Sheri to report what had happened. I sensed in my heart that I could not let the event remain unexposed, primarily because of my own weakness in this area. Further, I did not want the possibility of an ongoing temptation to lurk in my mind, or the picture of what I had momentarily seen to remain alive in my heart. I knew I had to step into the light of exposure immediately so the claws of temptation couldn't sink themselves into my flesh, and when I told Sheri what had happened, she prayed over me immediately on the phone, rebuked the enemy of our souls, and covered me with the blood of Jesus.

A couple months later, I was in a social setting with some acquaintances I hadn't seen in a while. As we sat and visited, their daughter stopped by. I was also acquainted with her, but hadn't seen her for several years. I immediately noticed that she had lost a considerable amount of weight and that she looked very nice. I was then surprised when she greeted me with a warm embrace. As we chatted for several moments, I could almost immediately sense the "vibe" all around her, and felt the strange but familiar feelings of sensual energy swirl around me. After we visited, she excused herself to the other room and disappeared accordingly. I completed my visit with her parents, and as I was getting ready to leave, they excused themselves to another room for several moments and their daughter returned to greet me. She told me how nice it was to see me again and extended her hand to me as if she wanted to shake my hand goodbye. As I reached for her hand and then took it, I told her goodbye, and what happened next is a little hard to explain, but I quickly realized in my heart that she was extending a kind of invitation to me as she continued to hold my hand and simply wouldn't let go for several extended moments. My mind raced ahead as the next couple moments passed as if in slow motion. I immediately felt the obvious presence of the "vibe," and like a lighting flash, I felt again a sense of sensual energy swirl all around the two of us. After an awkward moment, I pulled my hand away from her and quickly made my way to the front door. After saying goodbye, I began my drive home and began to cry. Although my tears felt cleansing, they were being offered from a trembling heart that feared such a close brush with a familiar enemy. Again, I relayed the entire event to Sheri later that same day, as I didn't want any level of temptation lurking secretly in the recesses of my heart or mind. Sheri prayed over me once again. Since that time I've had to push thoughts away from me on several different occasions when an invisible voice seems to remind me of this particular woman and whispers in my ear to remember her not-so-subtle invitation.

The final illustration of enemy fire I'll share is perhaps the most dangerous of all, and involves a particular couple that Sheri and I see regularly. As we have grown in our relationship with them, it is becoming more obvious that they struggle with some very real issues in their marriage — like we all do — and that this particular woman seems exceptionally lonely and vulnerable. Over the course of time, she has extended several flirtations and mildly suggestive overtures toward me, and at times I have suspected that she may have some level of infatuation with me. I talked to Sheri about my feelings and suspicions regarding this particular woman, and we agreed we would keep a careful eye on her. After Sheri and I agreed to watch this woman's behavior, we had the opportunity to be at a social event with her. As the evening drew to a close and people said goodbye, the woman approached me, touched me in a rather affectionate way, and kissed me on the cheek. Of course, Sheri was right next to me, and since we had already discussed the situation, her radar was in-tune and she was immediately suspicious of the inappropriate warmth that seemed to radiate toward me from this woman's heart. I say this may be the most dangerous situation because life circumstances require me to be around this woman regularly, and it's a relationship I cannot easily escape. Sheri and I have talked about this situation several times and I have asked Sheri and given her permission to keep a watchful eye on this woman when she is around me, and I have pledged to Sheri that I will do my best to stay out of her way and keep a watchful eye upon her. Although this is the kind of woman who would have spelled big trouble for me years ago, as the weakness that lived within me would have been easily tempted by her apparent vulnerability, I feel some sense of protection against her because of the place God has brought me to in my life and the level of honesty, communication, and accountability that now exists between Sheri and I.

I share these episodes of enemy fire in the attempt to convey as honestly as I can the reality of my ongoing battle and to give others the hope that victory over temptation is truly possible through the grace of God. I believe there is a very real enemy who would like nothing more than to totally destroy my life, my family, my testimony, and my ministry. He knows my weaknesses, does not give up easily, and has continued to fight to regain the power over my life that he used to enjoy for so long. In recent weeks, as I have neared completion of this book, Sheri and I have sensed increased spiritual attack against us on several different battlefronts. I believe in my heart that the enemy hates the idea of this book and in desperation has attempted to distract me from its completion through a parade of crazy and unexplainable events that seem to be going off around me like landmines. Although we know we are engaged in a very real battle, we also know and take confidence in the fact that we have been given authority over the kingdom of darkness. We are assured that we have been equipped with every good gift that enables us to walk in power and victory over our past and present temptations and trials that confront us. We know that ultimately we will triumph in complete victory over our adversary. We have read the Book, and we know the end of the story!

> And the devil, who deceived them, was thrown into the lake of burning sulfur, where the beast and the false prophet had been thrown. They will be tormented day and night forever and ever. Revelation 20:10

---

1 For the sake of absolute clarity and honesty, I feel compelled to explain that there have been a couple of occasions in the past 5 years when I have masturbated by myself, apart from my wife. These occasions occurred, for example, when Sheri was in Romania for an extended period of time on a mission trip. In advance of Sheri's absence, Sheri and I had discussed the problem of my physical pain and she gave me permission to masturbate, if I needed to, in order to eliminate such pain. Although I have masturbated apart from the physical presence of my wife on these rare exceptions, I believe I have continued to honor my vow before her and God because I did so only with her prior knowledge and permission. Since I renewed my vow, except for these few occasions, I have never expressed my sexuality apart from her physical presence and participation.

Chapter 39

Narrow is the Path

 I recognize that I am no expert on the subject of marriage, sexuality, masturbation, or the Bible. All I have to share with others is my personal story of struggle with both my sexuality and my God, and how God has worked in my life to deliver me from the chains of bondage that held me captive for so long. It is my hope that my story can serve as a kind of "mirror" for other men as they also struggle to honor God in this significant area of life. I believe there is no issue more central to being a man, or to masculinity, than the issue of sexuality, and that every single man struggles with this area to some degree. I believe this is an area of life that many men, including men in the Church, are struggling with in quiet desperation as they fail repeatedly and know in their hearts they are not being the men God has called them to be. Many men do not know how or where to go to find help for their struggle, since they are compelled to hide the shameful and embarrassing truth about their lives and failures. This is an area of life that desperately needs to be brought from the dark shadows that shroud it; shadows like silence, which allows us to ignore the reality of how deeply many men are struggling with their sexuality, and subterfuge, which allows many men to pretend they are doing better than they really are. The church desperately needs to deal with this issue head-on and allow forums and honest discussions that will create the opportunity for men to begin to move toward the "light" and to find honest answers that will lead them to freedom from chains of darkness and bondage. In addition, this topic needs to be brought from the shadows because I believe one of the greatest ways we can bring glory to God as men is to bring Him glory and honor through our sexuality. Surely God is glorified when we honor Him with our time, talent, and treasure, but I believe He is most glorified when we learn to honor Him from the deepest areas of struggle in our lives, where the rubber really meets the road, which for most men would include their sexuality. Since our sexuality is so central to what it means for us to be men, to bring glory to God through our sexuality is to bring glory to God from the deepest and most central place of our being.

One of the primary distinctions of Christianity from most world religions is that we believe we can have a personal relationship with God through and because of Jesus Christ. God is our Father and we are His children. We can know Him personally. We can fellowship with Him and we can hear His voice. He can and does speak to us. He leads us and guides us. He disciplines us and works in our lives in a very personal and unique way. He requires things of us and calls us into battle with Himself as He seeks to capture more of our hearts and make them His own.

Because of all these things, I cannot, and will not, try to tell other men what it means for them to honor God with their sexuality — that's between them and God as they stand, walk, and struggle with the reality of what their God is requiring of them. We do not need another man to mediate between God and us. We do not need the preacher to tell us what to do. We do not need an expert to tell us what is right. We do not need the most recent book to show us the way. Although all these things are good and they are tools through which God can speak to us and work in our lives, what we really need is our personal relationship with God. We need to talk to God, and hear from God, and struggle with God. We need to hear His voice and we need to obey whatever He requires of us. Because of these realities, I cannot tell you what it means for you to honor God in a greater way through the expression of your sexuality — that's between you and God. I know what it means for me to honor God with my sexuality, and I have a sense of what He has required of me as I have entered the arena to do battle with him. But I am not you, and you are not me. What He requires of me might be different than what He might require of you, and vice versa.

What I hope to do via this book is to encourage you, through the example of my story, to turn toward God — maybe more honestly than you ever have before — and to invite Him to show you whatever it is He wants to show you. Would you be willing to say something like this to God from your heart?

> Lord, I come to you and I lay my sexuality before you. I know what it is, and you know what it is. I'm asking you God to show me if you are pleased with how I express my sexuality. Is there something you want to say to me, God? Is there something you want to show me? Is there something you would require of me in this area of my life? Is there a way that you might be calling me to honor you, and to honor my wife (or girlfriend, for single guys), in a greater way through the expression of my sexuality? Are there things I need to repent of? Are there things I need to surrender to you? Are there steps I need to take in order to move toward the "light" of truth and freedom? God, I invite you to speak to me and to show me whatever you desire to show me.

I feel very strongly that if you would be willing to say a prayer like this to God, and mean it from your heart, that God will hear you and He will answer you. You certainly don't need me to tell you what you should or shouldn't do, and I might be wrong, but I suspect that since you have made it to this point in this book, that you may already hear the voice of God mysteriously calling to you as He is beginning to convict you in areas of your life where He, as the Master Surgeon, desires to accomplish deeper surgery.

I picture in my mind's eye a kind of scale from one to ten. Number one represents a man whose sexuality is in complete and absolute bondage and darkness. This guy is involved in the most reprehensible and sinister perversions and behaviors possible — like maybe he is a pedophile who has violently raped many children and is currently seeking his next victim. Or maybe he is a serial killer like Ted Bundy who stalks, abducts, rapes, and then kills women. On the other end of the scale, at number ten, is the most holy and righteous man possible. He is walking in complete freedom and victory in his sexuality, and he is honoring God completely. My guess is that most of us as Christian men are not at either end of the spectrum, but live somewhere on the continuum in between. One man might struggle with unnatural perversions like bestiality, pedophilia, or sadistic or masochistic behaviors. Another man might struggle with homosexual thoughts, tendencies, and behaviors, or frequently visit strip clubs, massage parlors, or prostitutes. The next man might struggle with continuously committing multiple adulteries, or have a major addiction to pornography or masturbation, or maybe he is involved in a single adulterous affair that has lasted for years, or he is having an emotional affair with a woman at work. The next man might only occasionally use pornography or masturbation, but his thought life is out of control as he continually consumes the women around him with his eyes and has an ongoing struggle with lust in his heart. Another man might wrongly be relating to his wife as more of a sex object to be used than a person to be loved, enjoyed, and cherished. You get the idea. But my challenge for you is that regardless of where you might be on this imaginary scale, that you honestly face where you stand and then ponder what it would mean and what it might look like for you to begin moving up the scale as you attempt to bring honor and glory to God in a greater way through your sexuality. You might compare yourself to guys on the lower end of the scale and therefore justify to yourself that you're not doing as bad as you could be. But I would encourage you not to minimize your sin in so doing, and to instead forget about where other men may or may not be and only compare yourself to what God might be asking of you.

Although it is not my intention to pontificate to you, or tell you what is right or wrong for you to do before God, I at least want to extend a challenge, specifically to those of you whom are married, for you to consider related to the subject of masturbation. I'm convinced that most men, including Christian men, continue to masturbate even after they are married, because most men I have talked to about the subject admit to struggling with this practice. I recognize that masturbation is a very controversial subject, even within the Christian community, and experts support almost any viewpoint on it. Great men of God, and men who know a lot more about the Bible and theology than I will ever know, differ greatly in their opinions and perspectives on the matter. God has used many of these men in great ways, and I'm sure they each love God deeply. Yet, they have arrived at greatly varied conclusions regarding the subject of masturbation, despite the fact that they all read the same Bible and pray to the same God.

Some people teach that masturbation is an acceptable practice because the Bible does not specifically say that it is wrong, as it does with fornication or adultery. They might suggest that masturbation is a common experience that the large majority of men practice, and it is therefore impractical to suggest that such behavior is wrong when so many people do it. I'm not sure I agree with such reasoning because I do not believe something should be determined as proper simply because a high percentage of people do it. For example, many people have premarital sex, have abortions, and practice homosexuality, but the fact that many people do so makes these actions neither right nor moral. We are called to a much higher standard than the plumb line of what the majority of people are doing or not doing. We are called to the standard of God's holy Word, and as image-bearers of God we are exhorted by Jesus to, "Be perfect, therefore, as your heavenly Father is perfect" (Matthew 5:48).

My primary concern, and thus my challenge for your consideration, revolves around my suspicion that many men use the convenience of masturbation, among other compulsive and addictive behaviors, to relieve themselves sexually and therefore avoid engaging their wives in real relationship. Don't ask me why God designed men and women the way He did, because in one sense it seems like a cruel joke, but that is the way God chose to do it. I recently received an email that poignantly illustrated the emotional and sexual differences between men and women. It was a picture of two different electronic instruments. One was labeled "Man," and simply contained a single on/off switch. The other was labeled "Woman," and the faceplate was covered with a complex and intricate system of dials, switches, lights, and gauges. It implies that while the man can be "turned on" with the flip of one lone switch, "turning on" the woman requires a complicated and endless procedure of tuning and fine-tuning in order to find and then maintain a signal. Ha! I think it's a funny metaphor because it contains such painful truth!

My point is that it takes a serious amount of consistent and concerted effort to get on the same wavelength with your wife and then stay there long enough in order to enjoy the delicious fruits of a healthy sexual relationship. You have to work really, really hard in order to be successful. You have to spend time together. You have to go on dates and go for walks. You have to talk and communicate. You have to understand her point of view and you have to learn to listen. You have to help around the house and with the kids. You have to learn to be sensitive, and you have to be understanding even when she's being emotional and she doesn't even understand what's going on inside of her. You have to face the music when she isn't happy about something in your relationship, or something about your life that has been bothering her, or something she thinks you need to change. You have to learn to not be defensive or self-protective. You have to learn to be sweet and kind. You have to do nice things like bring her flowers, wash the dishes, give her foot rubs, and remember what her favorite perfume is. You have to let her have time alone when she needs it, and you have to tell her "thank you" and open doors for her. You have to do all these things, and many, many more, and you have to do them all from your heart because you want to, because you love her more than anything else in your life, and not because you have to. If you happen to do them with a wrong heart or motive, she will somehow mysteriously and instantly know that something is out of place, she will not be free or responsive in how she relates to you, and you will have to start all over again as you attempt to win her heart and make it your own. In short, you have to be willing to die to yourself! "Husbands, love your wives, just as Christ loved the church and gave himself up for her to make her holy..." (Ephesians 5:25).

Apparently, in a strange mystery, as we learn to create such an atmosphere of warmth, tenderness, understanding, and unconditional love, we can then begin to enjoy the fruits of sexual intimacy our hearts truly long for.

But, alas, in the face of the challenging job description outlined above, which requires such continuous effort and self-denial, we are easily tempted to take the path of least resistance and turn to the convenience of masturbation. It's simply easier for us to "have sex" alone, and then take a nap, than it is to pursue our wives on a level that would require us to engage their hearts and win their passionate love. So instead we go to masturbation, pornography, the Internet, and a host of other false lovers in the vain attempt to satisfy our deepest longings, or we settle for body-to-body sex with our wives instead of pursuing the heart-to-heart sex God desires to bless us with. My challenge is therefore this: consider how you are using masturbation in your life. Are you using it as a convenient escape to avoid a true relationship with your wife — a relationship that could grow and prosper if you would face your wife and begin the difficult but rewarding journey of becoming a better man?

In my situation I think God was able to work far deeper in my heart and life when I made my vow to surrender masturbation, and that's why He required such a difficult step of obedience from me. I was worshipping masturbation as a false god in my life because it allowed me to avoid — through the convenient and momentary pleasure and escape it provided — the difficult realities of my past, my marriage, and my life. When I was required to surrender masturbation, I could no longer circumvent God's process of surgery in my heart. I was still a sexual creature, but since I could now only get sex from my wife, and not from myself, and was required to abandon the false lovers I had used for so long to satisfy myself, I was forced to turn toward my wife and engage her in deeper relationship than I ever imagined. As a result, I was forced to begin to deal with all the issues, problems, addictions, bondages, and chains that had lived in my life for so long.

In the end, I have a growing awareness of what a great and awesome "Warrior Poet" God really is, as He artfully drew me into battle and maneuvered me into the glorious places of defeat where He could begin to accomplish His purposes in my heart. If you think about it, God was masterful in the way He designed our wives to respond to us. They require so much of us, and God can use them in such a mighty way to make us better men — that's why I'm so concerned that we stop circumventing God's work in our hearts by turning away from our wives to our other false lovers, including masturbation.

I recognize that my challenge to you is difficult to consider. But I don't remember reading anywhere that living to God's standard is supposed to be easy. We are engaged in a very real war with very real enemies and very high stakes. We are exhorted in God's Word to control our bodies, rather than be controlled by our bodies, and we are encouraged to possess and offer our very bodies in sacrifice to God.

> Therefore, I urge you, brothers, in view of God's mercy, to offer your bodies as living sacrifices, holy and pleasing to God — this is your spiritual act of worship. Romans 12:1

> Do you not know that in a race all the runners run, but only one gets the prize? Run in such a way as to get the prize. Everyone who competes in the games goes into strict training. They do it to get a crown that will not last; but we do it to get a crown that will last forever. Therefore I do not run like a man running aimlessly; I do not fight like a man beating the air. No, I beat my body and make it my slave so that after I have preached to others, I myself will not be disqualified for the prize. I Corinthians 9:24–27

I'm sure the battle you might be called to face will not be an easy one, and I assure you my battle — as reflected through the "stories" in this book — has been anything but easy. But I'm equally sure the rewards will be far greater than you ever imagined as you journey down the narrow path and begin to enjoy the freedom and redemption of the Master Surgeon in your life, your marriage, and your sexuality.

Chapter 40
Sheri's Voice

Note: Tony's wife, Sheri, wrote this chapter.

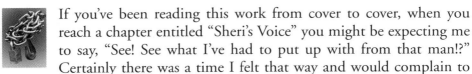 If you've been reading this work from cover to cover, when you reach a chapter entitled "Sheri's Voice" you might be expecting me to say, "See! See what I've had to put up with from that man!?" Certainly there was a time I felt that way and would complain to anyone who would listen. I often thought to myself, "If only Tony would change, then I could change." The details of what needed to change in our lives were insignificant until we were each willing to begin the process of first admitting we each needed to change. One woman who previewed Tony's chapters before editing and publication is reported to have become angry at Tony on my behalf. That's an understandable reaction, but I'm here to tell you that my husband has been painfully and courageously honest in these pages, which I respect and appreciate. To read my husband's words, full of compassion, acknowledging the ways I've been hurt, compels me to respond in kind. Even now I am keenly aware that I own an equal share of responsibility for the damage done to our marriage and to each other.

To those expecting to learn Tony and Sheri's secrets to a happy marriage, I'm sorry you have been sorely disappointed. Total repentance, flawless intimacy, and a cure for my aversion to sex remain illusive dreams for the future. So, is it really worth hearing my voice when we're still a couple plagued by our broken and fallen humanness? Can I offer you hope in the midst of life's difficult realities? This is my prayer. Although our marriage is not yet what we hope it will grow to be, there has been and continues to be an ever-increasing, gracious measure of healing, for which God alone gets the "blame."

It might be necessary to understand that many of the difficulties in my relationship with Tony began long before I met him. By the time I met Tony I had already become emotionally distant — not only because of the reasons he has already highlighted about my background — but partially because it is my natural tendency to withdraw from any difficult situation. Additionally, there are factors too numerous to include in one chapter.

To give you an idea of how I became so numb and emotionally disconnected from myself, it might help to know a bit more about my youth. As a teenager I felt compelled to have a boyfriend constantly, which gave me the secure "feeling" that I was special to someone who loved me. One boy in particular, a handsome and self-assured young man, made an impression on me and we began dating. I was drawn not only to his good looks but his cocky sense of self-confidence as well. Eventually we became engaged. This young man drew me into his family, but into a perverse lie as well. During our relationship he convinced me that he was actually dating below his station. He called me boring and stupid and said he should be dating a "smart, college girl." Many women might have told him to get lost, but I didn't. The way I let him treat me confirmed my already existent self-hatred. This is clear evidence to me that even as a teenager, I did not allow my emotions to be deeply touched by painful experiences.

Shortly before I met that boy, I became pregnant in the course of another ill-fated dating relationship. Almost as soon as I broke it off with that hot-tempered young man, I found out that I was pregnant. To his credit, he wanted me to have the baby and resume our relationship. However, within about 24 hours of learning I was pregnant, I had an abortion. I had never been confronted with the rightness or wrongness of abortion. To me it was just a solution to a dilemma. Through my experience at the clinic I was deceived and I felt — once again — worthless. Although the counselors were full of comfort and reassurances when I entered, a group of us were herded about like livestock, weeping, and then pushed through to make room for the next group of women entering. It wasn't until many years later that I understood those tears to be the beginning of a grief that I wouldn't revisit until after I became a Christian.

A much more profound and damaging event took place even before this abortion. I was raped when I was barely 14 years old. Many of you may be shocked when I tell you that I continued to date my attacker for the remainder of that summer. Others of you will understand perfectly how this could happen. My emotional nerves had been severed, plunging me into deep denial. It was as if on that night, in my neighbor's basement, my virginity was stolen from me and a switch was flipped that instantly darkened my soul. From that point on, until I became a Christian, I made all of my decisions as a person with little self-worth.

Now perhaps you have a better picture of the wounded and empty woman who met and married Tony, and my condition when I met Christ.

When I met Tony, I was especially drawn to his desire to find out all he could about me. He asked me questions that no one in my life had ever asked me before. He questioned me about my thoughts and feelings, about my past and who I was. Granted, I wasn't always able to answer his questions because I honestly didn't know much of what I thought or felt. All I knew was that it awakened a longing in me to be known, which I wasn't even aware existed. This stark contrast to being told I was boring and stupid quenched my thirsty soul.

My interest in Tony eventually grew into my desire to know God and understand the gospel. Even though it seems unfitting that a man involved in sexual sin would be presenting people with the gospel, it is clear evidence that God's power unto salvation is in the message rather than the messenger. In all fairness to Tony, he has never wavered, even to this day, in his desire to see people brought to God through the gospel. So in August, 1982, sitting on a lawn chair on my parents' driveway, Tony led me in the sinner's prayer. Just a little over a year later we were married.

During our engagement, Tony was dealing with the loss of his church, Canaan Bible Church. You have read that, in general, sexual misconduct led to the ministry's dissolution. Tony has long carried the burden of such public failure and shame. His shame was public because his ministry and position were public. There might be speculation on your part concerning why I stayed with him and was numb to such an obvious and public failure. You could assume I was just a very forgiving person — how gracious of you! Perhaps you are thinking I was too numb emotionally to have any kind of reaction. That's logical. However, I've given this some thought and I've narrowed it down to two fundamental reasons. First, I must make it clear that Tony treated me differently than any other man in my life ever had. Even after we became involved sexually, his interest in me as a person of worth remained. The fact that he had been sexually involved with other girls in his ministry wasn't enough of a reason for me to walk away from how much he valued me. Secondly, I felt as though I couldn't judge him because until shortly before we were engaged, I involved myself sexually with another man. I wasn't yet a Christian and, of course, my life wasn't in the limelight, but I understood the implications.

Immediately after we were married, something began to happen to me and it was very disturbing. Reading this now it seems like a no-brainer, but back then events seemed isolated and disconnected. On our honeymoon, I began to have a freakish sense during sex that I was being raped and an ugly, rageful, and murderous monster would well up in me. As soon as sex was over my rage would dissipate, leaving me feeling I must be insane. I soon realized that my marriage wasn't ever going to live up to my fairy-tale and dreamy expectations. I found myself alone — the object of my husband's anger and frustration — not knowing whom I could trust or confide in.

That was the state of affairs until that fateful day in March of 1995, when God rocked my world and shook me from the secure ground of my complacency. Despite my troubled marriage, I had found identity in my children, supervising the church nursery, and volunteering to deliver "Meals on Wheels." I even found a new joy in having a "best girlfriend." I never had girlfriends with whom I could do girl stuff. A new couple came into our circle of acquaintances and I became fast friends with the wife. She, my sister, and I embarked on a relationship that was new and refreshing to me. We went out to eat, saw "chick flicks" together, and commiserated about our annoying husbands. This new friend was the first visitor I laid eyes on in the hospital after our third son was born. When I learned that my husband had been having an on-again, off-again affair with her during our entire friendship, I felt far more betrayed by her than by my husband. The loss was devastating.

Over the next couple of years, through my counseling process, the deep freeze over my heart began to gradually thaw. I began to feel. And when I say feel, I mean FEEL! I got mad, I got radical, and the rush of pain that was rooted in my distant past culminated in a tidal wave of disappointment, anger, and self-hatred.

Of course, Tony has outlined our basic counseling arrangements, but the most profoundly life-changing benefit of all my years in counseling was my introduction to *The Wounded Heart* material by Dan Allender. This material, along with the group of women who made up my "safety zone," allowed me to long for more life and reconnect with my emotional self — without fear. With them I cried, grieved, laughed, and learned. I gathered courage from their love and acceptance. Never before had I been so transparent, but I knew these women would think no less of me if they knew the real me. I was right, and remain close friends with several of them to this day.

One night I was sharing with my Wounded Heart group about how I was responding to some "logs" God was trying to bring to my attention — logs in my own eye that needed to be confessed and submitted to God's healing touch. I explained that I continually averted my gaze from my issues and turned my head to point the finger of accusation toward Tony. "But God," I would complain, "What about him? Look at what he's doing!" I told them it was as if God was gently taking me by the chin and turning my head and eyes back to look at what I could change, rather than things about my husband that I couldn't change. The next morning I was walking through my house, not lifting, bending, twisting, or turning my head when I suddenly felt it…the divine "pinch." Something unseen literally "pinched" my neck and left me unable to even slightly turn my head to the left or right. I had often read a chapter in Dan Allender's book, *Bold Love,* called "Loving a Fool." As far as I was concerned it could just as easily have been called, "My foolish husband and how to survive being in a relationship with him." I picked up the book again since I could do little but sit on the couch. It opened automatically and easily to my husband's chapter. Suddenly, it occurred to me that I had never read the first ten chapters. How convenient! Convenient because in these earlier chapters, Allender discusses the need to deal effectively with our own sinful hearts before we seek to effect change in others. Could God really help me with my heart of criticism? Allender writes,

> I grew progressively silent in the light of what I saw in my heart, but if I had been asked about where I felt I failed my wife, I could have spoken of deep hurt. The key is that the silence that dawns in light of seeing your own sin does not discount the damage of others' sin. It simply puts it, for a time, in the background, where it waits to be addressed when your own heart is less disposed to judge and rage at another's failures. [1]

For years I wallowed in self-hatred because I felt utterly unworthy of the love and attention of others. But this is a far cry from what God wanted me to understand. Much worse than being a mere "innocent and unworthy bystander" in the catastrophe that was my life and marriage, I was actively responsible for hurting, damaging, and blaming those conveniently close to me. God did not need my self-loathing but rather longed for my repentance.

I mentioned how I became radical after I began thawing out and feeling more alive with God and others. I remember finding out about another woman being in our bedroom. Tony bought a new mattress and I took his credit card in order to purchase all new bedding and curtains. It felt good to assert my pain and He never once objected to the money I spent on linens. He knew I felt violated.

More aliveness followed. The freedom I experienced as a result of feeling, whether it was pain, sadness, anger, self-respect, joy, or honesty, was emboldening. Tony and I began to fight — I mean outwardly fight — for the first time in our marriage. In the past we would have "cold wars" where we wouldn't speak to one another for sometimes weeks at a time. I found fighting outwardly scary, and I even lost weight because my stomach was in a constant state of nervousness. At first Tony didn't appreciate my new-found "voice" or meeting with such strong resistance from me outside the bedroom. This was new territory for both of us. So it is a startling picture of God's gracious invasion into our marriage that the very man who once wanted to silence my voice has now invited me to be heard in a book about his wounded sexuality.

Over the last 9 years, we have alternated between working together as a team to heal our marriage and frequently attempting to briefly escape our strained marriage. Think about it. We were emotionally beating up each other with an exhausting passion, because we just knew if we stopped for even a moment, our own shortcomings would be revealed. Under such circumstances, what husband wouldn't prefer a game of golf? What wife wouldn't enjoy her husband leaving on a hunting trip? So often my husband retreated to the guest bedroom in the basement because it was too painful to lie in bed next to someone who didn't accept him and couldn't forgive. Sometimes his escape became my relief, and in this way we prolonged our healing just like wounded people are apt to do. Today, Satan no longer deceives us into thinking we need to escape from one another, because we are instead each learning to accept responsibility for ourselves and to own our own shame when we fail.

The final turning point that helped my husband and I to move toward one another was a serious breach in fellowship between my husband and his father, along with his father's sudden death 2 years ago. When Tony was struggling to assert his adulthood and establish boundaries with his father, we became more of a team as we worked through this difficult situation together.

As my husband has been writing this book, chapter by chapter and story by story, he has literally been revisiting his past and had to stare his sin in the face. He has responded humbly, reading chapters to me through repentant sobs. As in the beginning of our relationship so it is now. Tony offers me something unique and treasured that no man ever offered: an ever-deepening understanding of God's power to save and his loving desire to rescue.

As for the future, only God knows, but I know that no matter what comes — whether natural disasters, persecution, war, or even marital discord — our God, the God Tony introduced me to 22 years ago, is able to deliver us! We appreciate your prayers.

---

1 *Bold Love,* Dan Allender, NavPress, 1993, page 70.

Tony Ingrassia is an author, speaker, pastor, and entrepreneur. After becoming a Christian as a teenager, he studied for ministry at Florida Bible College, where he was elected student body president and graduated in 1979. Tony earned his Master of Arts in Counseling (M.A.C.) at Covenant Theological Seminary in 2007. Tony is currently a pastor at Discovery Church in St. Peters, Missouri. He also operates Freedom Counseling Service, where he specializes in helping men who are struggling with issues of sexual purity. Tony has authored the following books concerning sexual purity: *Stories, The power of Purity,* and *The Power of Purity Workbook.*

Tony is an entrepreneur who has worked in the remodeling, real estate, and consulting industries. In 1987 he started his own remodeling company and grew it into one of the largest Midwest companies of its kind. After selling that company in 1996, he authored various programs designed to help other home remodeling companies improve their business processes and increase their profits.

Tony lives in St. Charles, Missouri with his wife and their three sons. He owns a farm in northern Missouri, which allows him to pursue his other interests, including hunting, fishing, and enjoying the great outdoors.

Tony can be contacted for further information through his website:

www.powerofpurity.org

Helping Men Honor God Through Sexual Purity

The Power of Purity: Freedom From the Roots of Sexual Sin

There is no issue more central to masculinity than the issue of sexuality, and it represents one of the most common and deepest struggles for many Christian men. Although Christian men know they are called to sexual purity, many find it difficult to achieve as they struggle with various manifestations of sexual sin, including an impure thought life, masturbation, pornography, and the internet, among other things. Many men are simply incapable of overcoming the sinful tendencies they have struggled with for so long, and are powerless to break free from the invisible chains that hold them in places of captivity. Why are so many good men struggling so deeply with their sexuality? Why do so many men find it impossible to put their sexual struggles behind them and move into higher levels of sexual purity? *The Power of Purity* answers these questions along with many others.

The central message of this book can be reduced to the simple phrase, "fruit comes from roots." Fruit is always the result of roots, and if a man is struggling with the ongoing manifestation of sexual sin, it is typically because of unholy sexual "roots" that have never been properly addressed. A man attempting to live in sexual purity, who has never dealt with these unholy roots, would be like an apple tree no longer producing apples: impossible. As long as unholy roots remain, unholy fruit will follow. *The Power of Purity* clearly exposes the six unholy roots common to Christian men, and invites the reader into a process of repentance that will renounce the power and break the authority of each root in his life. Sexual purity does not have to remain a hopeless and unachievable dream. God has given the Christian man all things that pertain to life and godliness, and with His help sexual purity is truly possible.

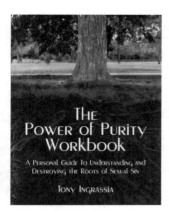

The Power of Purity Workbook: A Personal Guide to Understanding and Destroying the Roots of Sexual Sin

There's a saying that the definition of *football* is: 22 men who desperately need rest, playing a game in front of 50,000 men who desperately need exercise! This definition reminds me of Christianity because Christianity is not designed as a spectator sport. God intends for every man to "get in the game," and that is the very purpose of *The Power of Purity Workbook*. It's not good enough to just read books about sexual purity. It's not good enough to just read books or attend conferences about sexual purity. Although these are good initiatives, ultimately each man needs to "get in the game" and begin to apply the principles of sexual freedom to his own life and walk the pathway of repentance God has designed for him. This workbook provides a man, or preferably a small group of men, a practical and tangible way to apply the principles of sexual freedom to their very own lives. *The Power of Purity Workbook* will walk men through the step-by-step process of repentance that will release the power of God into their lives to bring the freedom, release, and healing they are seeking.